Workbook

By
Claudia Haltom

Keith Publications, LLC
www.keithpublications.com
©2013

Arizona
USA

I

THE SINGLE PARENT REFEREE WORKBOOK

By Claudia Haltom

Cover art by Elisa Elaine Luevanos
www.ladymaverick81.com

Cover art Keith Publications, LLC © 2013
www.keithpublications.com

ISBN: 978-1-936372-98-0

If you are interested in purchasing more works of this nature, please stop by
www.keithpublications.com

Contact information: info@keithpublications.com
Visit us at: www.keithpublications.com

Printed in The United States of America

Dedication
To Billy, the love of my life.

Acknowledgements

Inspiration for *The Single Parent Referee* came from seventeen years as a judicial referee with the Shelby County Juvenile Court in Memphis, Tennessee. During those seventeen years I witnessed every variation on the theme of dysfunctional families and terrible parenting. In spite of that, the greatest inspiration also came from the families who worked together and made the best of difficult situations. As a judicial referee I witnessed and judged parents and family members take a worst case scenario and come out of it with amazing children, positive lives and lots of love. It can happen.

Watching hundreds of examples of the best and the worst in people from the judge's side of the bench, I have written this book and all of its stories with no specific cases or people in mind. None of the examples represent real individuals, rather they are all samples of many issues and many stories combined.

Witnessing such extremes in parenting and relationships gave me a renewed appreciation for the love of my life, the man to whom I am dedicating this book. My husband Bill has encouraged me and supported me for thirty years. He has been my greatest promoter as well as my number one booster. He is the real writer in the family, with four books published and another on the way. I also want to thank the other men in my life, all of whom have been loving, kind and encouraging. My dear father has taught me lessons of hard work, perseverance and kindness. He would tell me to use praise words to encourage other people. He taught my big brother how to treat his little sister and how to look out for and help me. My father and brother were the first men whom I learned to love and admire. They set the standard and created the mold that helped me choose my husband.

Next, I dedicate this book to my incredible sons and daughter. These wonderful boys, who are now fine men, have always been respectful, always tried to please and always made me proud, and my blessed surprise, my gift from God, the grace we didn't expect or deserve is my daughter. She is made in the image of her grandmothers. She is so like both of them. The tradition continues.

My editor Nicholson Hitching helped me pull these stories together. Nicky is a wonderful writer and fabulous organizer. This book is a compilation of many lives and many lessons with no story being unique. Parents can learn from the lessons and mistakes of others. Nicky is the best editor possible.

Another wonderful writer, encourager and role model is Dawn LaFon. She has taken all my ideas and helped me mold them into much more than a work in progress. She has pushed me to keep on and finish the job.

Table of Contents

INTRODUCTION
What to Do When It's Just You

This is a workbook about planning a family you never planned.

Being a single parent is real. That wonderful little boy or girl, that toddler or teen is all yours and sometimes, yours alone. Scary wonderful. Scary alone. The trip you're about to make together is the journey of a lifetime. It can be a great one.

Throughout this workbook you'll find:

- **REFEREE'S RULES** to help you quickly reference what you should and should not do as a single parent.

- **PRACTICAL TIPS** to help with parenting.

- **TALKING TIPS** to help you know what to say and when to say it.

- **LEGAL TIPS** to help you prepare and know where to go.

You will also find plenty of first person stories from single parents and their families. Some are just like you and some have very different perspectives on the challenges that single parents face.

Raising kids is a trip.

Raising kids without being married to your child's parent will take you down a path that has few, if any, rules. By planning with this workbook, you'll have a map for keeping that journey in the middle of the road, out of the ditches on either side, and aware of the twists and turns ahead when you and the other parent are apart.

How do you survive the diaper years and eventually have a teen you can stand to be around?

Both parents can be on board and stay cool.

Mom and dad don't have to be together to give their kids comfort and security. This workbook is for single parents. Some live with their kids and some don't, but all want to be involved in their kids' lives. They know their kids need both parents. At times you might feel cut out. You may have been excluded for any number of reasons, but now you want to be there. This workbook will give you direction for all of these situations. It will also help both parents get prepared if and when they face legal matters.

A little help from our friends.

This workbook is also for the people who love, help or advise parents who are not married. You might be the counselor, minister, teacher, aunt, grandparent or lawyer of these moms and dads. You see that they aren't sure where to begin or where things will end. You want to help out and this workbook can show you how.

Doing nothing gets you nowhere, so know your options.

The key is to know what will happen if you do nothing versus what will happen if you make certain choices. Know the outcome of choices and use this workbook to understand practical and legal options. Use this workbook to learn the practical and legal options of those choices. Through stories you can see examples of problems and how other moms and dads work through them. Learn what information counts. Know your options. Then, keep track of what you have learned through this workbook.

How can this workbook help?

First, this workbook will share typical stories to help you decide what you really want.
Hearing other single parents' stories will help you decide what you want and don't want for you and your child.

Second, this workbook will help you plan for change and put together all of the information that matters.
Look at your options, know that things WILL change. Kids turn into teenagers. Adults marry, re-marry and move. By understanding what changes are likely to come, you can plan what to do when it happens.

Third, this workbook will go over the ten biggest problems faced by a mom and dad who never married or are divorced. How do you avoid or cope with these potholes?
Some of these problems might not fit your life. More importantly, some of the solutions might fit. Always remember this is a workbook, not a cookbook or an instruction manual. It will help you find your way to raising a great kid.

Most importantly, this is a workbook. So, go to the Appendix and print out your workbook pages if you want to hand write your journal, or go to the website www.singleparentreferee.com for self-help resources and other tools.

Let's get started. Go to Chapter One, *What to Do About You.* Wait! Maybe you are still not convinced. If not, keep reading. Perhaps you want to disappear or you want the other parent to vanish. Just pretend this will go away. Maybe? *Big mistake!*

Before we start, maybe you're at another place. Avoidance. You think, "Do not stir the pot or it will create problems." Denial. The kid does not exist. The other parent does not exist. If this is where you are, you are headed for disaster. This approach will come back to haunt you in a number of ways. The lid will not stay on this situation for eighteen years. Here are just a few of the problems from all sides that can result from the avoidance method of parenthood:

- Your child will want to know about the missing parent and will long for a relationship with that parent.

- Your child may idealize this absent parent as somebody wonderful whom you are hiding from him and blame you for the absence.

- Your child will always resent you if you are the missing parent.
- Your child will turn into this incredible person and you will truly regret having missed it all.

- Your child will have major emotional problems and blame you for all of it.

- When the missing parent starts showing up it will create drama. Drama results in bad scenes.

- Your future marriage and family life will be damaged.

- Who will care for you in your old age? A bad nursing home.

- Nobody respects deadbeat parents.

- Avoiding child support can mess up your finances permanently. You can get hit with child support back to birth. It can be collected through garnishment of your paycheck for years, a lien on your bank account or a lien on your house or any lawsuit where you have received money. A penalty can include a forfeiture of any license (like a drivers license, real estate license, commercial drivers license, professional license, fishing and hunting license or passport). The IRS can even intercept your tax refund.

- Child support arrears are subject to interest of 12% per year in many states. Did I mention when you have child support arrears (debt you owe from not paying in the past) you cannot even get a passport?

How would I know? I have seen it happen over and over again. As a juvenile court judicial referee for seventeen years, I have heard literally thousands of cases involving families in which the parents never married or were divorced. I have seen the magic that can happen when parents commit themselves to being great parents. Unfortunately, I have seen the heartbreaking consequences when they don't. You have the power to make a difference and this workbook will show you how. Here's our first story.

I've always known my father was a prominent doctor in our small town. Mom would point him out to me when we would see him on the street. He would nod at her and stare at me. I suppose he was looking for that glimpse of similarity between me and his other daughter, who was usually with him when he was in town. It was there, all right. We both had the same shade of auburn hair, the same stocky but not heavy frame and the same round but not flat nose. She went to the Catholic girls' school in town, I went to the local public school. She went away to camp in the summer or to Europe with her mother. I worked for a day care in the summer. She got a car for her sixteenth birthday. I can't even remember what I got for my sixteenth birthday. When it came time to go to college, his daughter went away to a small, expensive, private liberal arts college. Mom asked him to pay my tuition to the community college. He said, "No." So, a month before my eighteenth birthday, Mom filed for child support against my dad, going back eighteen years. Wow, she blew the lid off. I was so proud of her. She held her head high for me. She did it all for me. Wow, she got the money!

CHAPTER ONE

What to Do About <u>You</u>
The Starting Point for Your Journey is Your Story

All children's lives happen in phases that I call milestones. This helps you see what is coming down the road. Look around the curve and anticipate danger. Below are some childhood milestones to consider. The stone that marked the end of every mile in olden times, like the little green signs on the interstate, let people know not only how far they had come but also how much further they had to go. As you go through this workbook, it helps to look at your child in terms of three-year milestones. Think of your child now, then in three years, then three more years, then three more. This is predicting the future and also dealing with the consequences, both good and bad. You get the idea.

So, who are you and what is your story? Where does it start and where will it end? Below are the milestones for each era of a child's life. Pick your spot based on the age of your child or ages of your children. (For the rest of this book, I will refer to one child, but the stories work for multiple children also.) That is usually where your story begins for planning purposes. However, we all know your story really began well before this. Now, start at your child's milestone below.

- **Birth to age three:** The baby years. These are stressful for all new parents. Focus on stable, safe childcare if both parents work. Cuddle and read and sing. Let grandparents, aunts or uncles help.
- **Ages three to six:** The pre-school years. Have a schedule and create a stable structure. Have your child in kindergarten or some pre-school program. Reading is the educational focus. Counting is important.

- **Ages six to nine:** The critical first three years of school, with first grade a huge milestone. Reading and writing are important. A lot of moving during these years is very disruptive and difficult for a child. Just be real. Be yourself.
- **Ages nine to twelve:** The pre-teen years. Sports skills are developing and math skills need a strong base. If math is not strong, get math help. Try out a sports team and musical training. Something might stick. Don't try to be perfect, just do your best and they will, too.
- **Ages 12 to 15:** Often the drama years. The first year of high school is a critical milestone. It is vital for that year to be thought-out, planned and begun in a stable environment. Your child needs strong friends. This is where the sports team or musical group will give him or her a friend base. Feed those activities.
- **Ages 15 to 18**: The survival years. Your teen will pull all of the same stunts you and your friends may have pulled, plus some. Look out for drinking, smoking, sex and drugs. Talk about this and put your prevention plan in place. Plan for college. Pray. Listen.

These milestones can help you direct your plan. However, your story and the other parent's story are what you use to create your plan.

- **REFEREE'S RULE:** Get stability in your life.

- **PRACTICAL TIP:** Take yoga or some other exercise program.

- **TALKING TIP:** Learn to say, "I could use some help with… please."

- **LEGAL TIP:** Make sure the dad is listed on the birth certificate. This is called legitimating the child or being the legal father.

Now here are some mini stories. One of these might be you.

It was never about love, it was always about sex. We didn't have the kind of relationship where you get married, much less have a BABY. We weren't ready for anything permanent. We certainly weren't ready for THIS. We did not want to be parents. Now we have a baby!

***

We were best friends, not lovers. Then, we just started adding the "benefits" but we were still just friends. This does not make a family… but I'll be there. I think she thought it was more.

***

We dated steadily but always argued and I was ready to move on. I had already found my next true love and just needed to break this off. Having a baby will so mess up my next love. I really want to ignore this and hope it will go away. I can't make a decision or a commitment on anything. I will avoid this "situation."

***

I don't have enough money for myself, much less a child. This is all so expensive. I just don't have the money.

***

We've had some really bad scenes and I think he/she is crazy. I don't want to ever see him/her again. He/she totally creeps me out. Scares me, really.

***

When I saw my child, everything changed.

***

When I saw my child, I didn't feel a thing. Is bonding supposed to be automatic? It didn't happen to me.

When I told him I was pregnant, he looked like I had slapped him. He never asked if I was okay or how did I feel. He finally said, "Are you sure that I am the dad?" That's when I felt like I had been slapped. I'll never get over that. I play that scene over and over and over in my mind.

You've got to be brutally honest with yourself.

Honestly and privately, tell yourself how you feel about being a parent with this person who is the other parent. Don't feel bad or guilty. It is what it is. Own your feelings. Acknowledge your strengths and weaknesses. This book will help you learn to overcome your weaknesses. Play to your strengths. This is not a guilt trip but a road trip for your life. This will only work if you are honest with yourself. Any of the above stories could be your story. They are just there to help you get started.

It is not easy to own up to those feelings and this workbook requires you to go the extra mile and actually write them down. As a single parent, your time is precious, but you will need to give some of it up for what I am asking you to do. Set aside an hour *or longer* and make sure you have paper and pencil, your computer or tablet. Sit down and get ready. If you get to a question that sets you off, take a separate piece of paper and write until you tell your story. Don't worry about it making sense to anyone else. It's for you. Then you can decide what to put down as your workbook answer to the questions below. If you don't finish before your time is up, go ahead and set aside some more time later on. You can hand write this on your Appendix work pages or go to www.singleparentreferee.com for your online resources and workbook tools. This is "Your Story."

Starting Point
Before you decide where you're going,
you need to know where you are.

Let's start with a single parent inventory. Before you decide where you want to go, it's time to write down where you are. So set aside your hour, and get ready. Remember, it is only going to help you if you are completely honest. *Who* you are and *where* you are going are different parts of the same story. The questions below will lead you further into *your* story.

> *I have a college scholarship out of town. If I don't take it, none of my goals for my life will ever be met. The other parent deserves to go to college, too, but this is my only opportunity to get a scholarship. I have to go.*

***

> *I always lose my temper about something. My temper gets me into so much trouble. Frustration boils up so quickly. I've said lots that I regret and I've torn up a lot of things when I've been angry. What kind of parent can I be when I get angry so easily?*

***

Now, look yourself in the mirror and find the good and the not-so-good. This book is going to help you look ahead. In five years or fifty-thousand miles, will you have arrived at a good place or will your life be up on blocks in the same old place? Will you be headed in the right direction or swerving all over the road? As you go through this workbook, think five years out, then ten years. Or if your child is only a baby, you better go eighteen years out, maybe more, since in eighteen years your child may still be in high school. You are responsible until then. Now, use these questions to direct your story.

Remember to answer these questions with what is really real, not what you *want* to be real. (These questions are in the Appendix A, "Your Story".)

<u>Your</u> Story: Who are you? Where are you right now?

1. What are your strengths and weaknesses as a person and as a parent? This is your best and worst stuff. Examples:
> "I have lots of energy."
> "I can stroll for hours."
> "I can coach soccer or baseball."
> "I am a good cook."
> "I'm great with animals."
> "I also have a bad temper and no patience."
> "I get bored and annoyed easily."

2. What do you like to do in your free time? With your child, then without your child. Examples:
> Go to the playground.
> Go to movies.
> Watch TV.
> Watch sports.
> Hang out with friends.

3. Are you happy with your job/career choice? Have you had setbacks? Examples:
> "I'm still in school, but with the wrong major."
> "My job went out of business."
> "I really don't want to work."

4. What do you want to be doing in five years? Ten years? Examples:
> Own a business.
> Finish nursing school.
> Get a college degree.
> Get licensed as an electrician.

5. What will it take for you to make your goal? Examples:
> Go back to school.
> Pay off debts or student loans.

6. What changes do you intend to make on the career front? How and when? Is this realistic? Example:
> "I want to go to law school, but I made bad grades."

7. Is your housing stable? Is it a good place for your child? Does he or she have a room? Bed? Toys?

8. Who do you live with? Is this good for your child? Will this person help you reach your goals?

9. Have there been any domestic violence scenes with you or with the other parent?

10. Have the police ever been called to your house for fighting? Should they have been called?

11. Who is your support network? List each person in your network by name and number.

12. What are you most proud of?

13. How long have you been involved with the other parent?

14. How many children do you have? How many does he/she have?

15. What bothers you the most about parenting?

16. What is the main problem involving the other parent? Can this be fixed or must you learn to live with it? Examples:
> "She is married to someone else."
> "He is in prison for the next five years."
> "She picks a fight at every visitation drop off."
> "She never gets our child to school on time."

17. Do you have bitterness or resentment that you cannot get over? What and why? (Use extra paper if necessary.) Example:
> "He or she used me, abused me, mistreated me, lied to me."

18. Do you want the other parent involved a lot? A little or not at all? Is this with you or with the child? Do YOU really want the other parent back? Examples:
> "We can co-parent this child apart."
> "I never want to see him/her again."
> "I really want to get back together with the other parent. "

19. Have you caused hurt or mistrust that needs to be cleared up? How?

20. Have you said things that have caused major problems?
Example:
> "I told him he was not the dad, that his best friend was the baby's dad. It was not true."

21. Is there a negative pattern about your life that needs work?
Example:
> "I always get involved with people at work and it messes up the job."

22. What are the really good things going on with your kids?
Example:
> "They are doing great in school."

23. How does the rest of the family fit into the picture?
Example:
> "My parents are very, very helpful/critical/unhelpful."

24. Is your childcare good? Is your child happy? (More on this later.)

25. Keep writing the rest of your story.

Tune up your inventory.

As you discover more about where you are, you may realize things are basically good but there can be improvement, which will help make everyone happier. If your inventory of where you are causes you to feel your life is not in a good place, then it is time to make some changes. Try to figure out how to get where you and your family want and need to be.

Do you have personal shadows or secrets you need to deal with? Pornography, illegal drugs, alcoholism, gambling, shop lifting/bad checks and dishonesty are all shadows that will eventually come out and will impact you as a person and as a parent. Do not avoid or deny your shadows. Face them, list them and promise yourself you will deal with them. Are you at a place with these shadows where you need help? Professionals are committed to helping people with these problems in a confidential manner. Professional counselors in any of these areas must keep your secrets and help you overcome your problems. Seeking help is a significant step in proving you have changed. Here are two examples:

She and I met at a strip club. She was a dancer and I was a regular customer. I tipped well; she re-paid the tip. When she got pregnant and insisted I was the father, naturally I wanted a DNA test and she completely understood. Now I know the kid is mine. The court set child support. I wanted visitation, but I wanted more. Heck, my baby's momma was a hooker. I wanted custody. At the hearing I could completely prove her career and place of employment, but she showed up with proof she had been in a rehabilitation program for porno dancers. I was still a regular customer. She had started school, gotten another job and been going to counseling for self-esteem, along with parenting classes. Now I was the one who looked so bad.

***

I have this bad habit of shop-lifting. It started in high school when I would go to the mall with friends. We never got caught because we were always in private school uniforms. Now I just do it for kicks. A baby stroller or a diaper bag is the best cover ever. Of course, if I get caught stealing with my child, I could lose custody. My ex is just waiting for that opportunity. He would jump at the chance to humiliate me like that. He is out to get me. But, I can't stop stealing. I need help.

***

- **REFEREE'S RULE:** Be honest with yourself.

- **PRACTICAL TIP:** Don't beat yourself up with your weaknesses.

- **TALKING TIP:** "I am going to create a positive plan."

- **LEGAL TIP:** Getting professional help will usually not make things worse in court. Needing help but not getting it will always work against you.

CHAPTER TWO

What to Do When You Don't Really Know What to Do
The Trip in Four Not-So-Easy Steps

The first step: Figuring out what you really want.

Now that you know who and where you are, let's figure out what you really want. In family matters what you think you want in the beginning may not be at all what you realize you want in the end. Be honest with yourself. Is one of these "gets" really your true goal?

- **Getting out of paying child support.**

- **Just getting more money from the other parent.**

- **Getting even with the other parent.**

- **Getting control of everyone I hate.**

If one of these is your goal, you've got the wrong book. This is about children, not furniture, cars, houses or bank accounts. This is NOT a *Revenge for Dummies* book.

This is a self-help workbook and website (www.singleparentreferee.com) to help *you* as a single parent deal with the issues unique to your parenting situation.

The first question you must honestly answer is: What do you really want? Be careful what you pray for because you just might get it. What will you really do if you get what you ask for? Do you have a plan, or is this really about money and ego? We are talking about children who look, act and think like their parents. These children will grow up to become the people who will ultimately call you when you are old and lonely, show up when you are sick, come for all holidays (or not), blame you for their dysfunctional, screwed-up lives, and finally, pick out your nursing home.

Children are not objects for revenge or pawns for power play. For your own self-preservation, if for no other reason, your goal should be to be a good, kind, attentive parent and your children will usually follow your example. When you are old, they are likely to treat you exactly as you have treated them.

As you move down the road from where you are now to where you want to be, this is all about what is best for your kids in a plan that will work with your life.

- **REFEREE'S RULE:** You never get what you want unless you know what it is.

- **PRACTICAL TIP:** If your life is not stable, this part might be difficult. Don't give up.

- **TALKING TIP:** "What time is best for you?" "Really, let's be specific. How can I help out?"

- **LEGAL TIP:** Try to work out a compromise and mediate with the other parent. Go to court only as a last resort. Court action can take you places you really don't want to go. It can bring out the worst in everyone.

By knowing what you want, you can map out your plan more successfully. When what you want changes, that's okay. It is normal for plans to change when you are raising kids. The children's needs change, and your life and relationships will change. Yet, this will always be your child. To help you get moving, the next section will lead you to write down on paper or log on your computer or tablet what you truly want in custody, parenting time and relationships regarding your child. Let's get back to our goal of figuring out what you want.

Put aside the anger and resentment toward the other parent. Think only about you and your child and how you can give that child love and support. Think of your child now, then in three years, then three more years, then three more. It might help to go back to the chart at the beginning of Chapter One that lists these three-year milestones.

Most parents want and need time with their child, time that fits in with their work, school and social life. Parents want and need help with all of the pick-ups and drop-offs in a child's schedule. Having a weekend or weekday off from the relentless task of parenting is also a nice break, provided you know your child is happy and safe.

Dividing a child's activities between parents and grandparents based on what everybody really likes is the best way to divide up the parenting responsibilities. If dad played a high school sport, then he might be the best parent to be in charge of sports. Grandparents often want to be helpful with church. You don't have to be a super-parent, so don't try to compete with the other parent by always being present when the other parent is supposed to be responsible. Give yourself a break and give the other parent a chance. Consider these examples:

My dad was my basketball coach and I loved it. I want to coach my child, too. I want to help pick a school where I can help with his sports and be a coach. I want to be able to take him to college games and show him big-time sports stuff. He can be in his mom's custody, but I want to be very involved.

***

My daughter is ten. I just married a great guy who is in a band and wants me to travel a lot with him. I want joint custody with her dad, but I want to travel a lot with my new husband. I want the dad to keep her but when I am home I want her to come to my place. During the summer I want her to be able to travel with us.

***

She was really wild when we dated. Since the baby was born she has not slowed down one bit. She still parties all of the time. When I see her friends, they all tell me how cute our baby is because they have seen our baby at their parties. Now, that's just wrong. I've settled down a lot and I want full custody. A baby should not be a toy at her mother's wild parties. My ex should only have visits with our baby when they are supervised by someone responsible.

***

As you think about what you want, make this a rough draft. Don't forget the milestones. Think about where your child will be at those three-year points. You will probably throw away or delete your first version regarding your plans. Then, you will change your mind as you consider all of the options.

Before you start, think about custody, now and in the future. Things will change. Whenever possible, have *joint* custody with one parent being the primary residential guardian. As life changes and you face the different milestones, you can change which parent is the primary residential guardian without having a huge custody fight. Next, think about parenting time or visitation, both yours and theirs. What about extended family? Grandparents? What do you really want?

You don't have to know everything. But please, don't fake your goals. This is about what you really want based on the life you have or plan to have. This is about planning to have a relationship with your child, a real little person, who will have opinions and attitudes about life. Chances are this little person will be a lot like you. This little person will act just like the folks in your family. You should be more honest right now than you have ever been in your life.

Below are the questions to answer so you can figure out what you want: (These questions, along with answer space are in Appendix B, "What you Really Want," or online at www.singleparentreferee.com.)

1. Describe in detail what parenting time/visitation schedule you want regarding your child and the other parent or his/her family.

2. List what you think you want to DO with your child. How much time do you want to spend with your child? Now? In the future? Remember those three year milestones.

3. When do you need a break? (For example, every Friday night, or maybe Sunday afternoons?)

4. How involved do you want to be with their activities? Really?

5. What educational/child care decisions do you want to make? For example, what school should your child attend?

6. Look ahead at least one milestone (three years) and see how you think things might change. What school changes might there be? Will you or the other parent be engaged or married?

7. What holidays are important to you and your family? Consider if you work during Christmas and need help during the holidays.

8. What family events matter to you and your family? For example, claim the week of your family reunion if it is important to you that your child be part of that celebration.

9. What is your work schedule? School schedule? Study schedule? When will it change?

10. What is your child's schedule?

11. Does your child have any unique needs?

12. What is the other parent's schedule?

13. What family members are available and dependable?

- **REFEREE'S RULE:** Joint custody with one parent being the primary residental guardian is a very good plan.

- **PRACTICAL TIP:** Joint custody doesn't work if parents cannot get along.

- **TALKING TIP:** "Can we do this together?"

- **LEGAL TIP:** Obtain joint custody in a court order. If it is not in a court order, it does not count. Consider these stories:

I have just been offered a great job one thousand miles away. I really want to take this job. I really love my child. How can I do this?

***

I want to be a real parent who talks with their kid every day or every other day. I want to be able to take him with me to movies and family reunions. I want him to go to my mom and dad's church, at least for Easter. I want to be the one he calls when he has big news to tell or needs help or gets lonely. However, I want him to live at the other parent's house.

***

My wife does not know about this outside child. I don't intend to tell her. I will pay my child support, but I just can't do any more.

***

I need my parents to help me deal with this. I've just joined the military.

***

I want full custody because she only wants this child to try and get money from me and the government. It could be: I want full custody because he is just trying to get out of paying child support.

***

I live out of town, so the other parent can make all of the school decisions. I have no idea what schools are good in that city.

21

**

It is very important to me that my child go to the school where I went. My brother's children go to that school, and I know I can count on my old teachers to always look out for our child.

**

- **REFEREE'S RULES:** Do not try to compete with the other parent. Do not try to avoid being a parent.

- **PRACTICAL TIP:** Get ready to do exactly what you ask for. Rearrange your job schedule. Get your family to help.

- **TALKING TIP:** "We've got a great new plan..." Build your child up to accept and be happy with what you have put together.

- **LEGAL TIP:** Without a court order you have nothing to enforce. Without a court order you can only make things happen if you always agree. That is unlikely to happen in the best of relationships. Avoid misunderstandings. Get a court order confirming everything you have agreed upon.

- **LEGAL TIP:** Try to have a consent order where you both agree.

If you can both agree on everything, then you can have a consent order. Usually this takes give and take. You might feel like you are the only one giving. It is worth it to finalize things and not argue. A consent order is an order where you both agree upon all the details and it is entered with the court without any disagreement or trial. Often only a lawyer presents it in court, but it is still a court order that everyone must follow. Make sure you understand it all. Make sure it is signed by a judge. Keep your copy in a safe place.

The second step: Getting through your issues.

The social and emotional issues need to be dealt with just like the legal issues. In fact, they are often the toughest issues of all. There are really only four legal issues: paternity, child support, parenting time/visitation and custody. (Skip to Chapter Nine for more about these legal issues.) There can be social and emotional issues that are much more numerous and tougher than legal issues. If you do not put them into their proper perspective and deal with them, these issues can block you from acting in your child's best interest. These hang-ups, no matter how justified, can cause you to want to get even more than you want to get child support. These hang-ups can cause you to want revenge more than you want success. Resentment, jealousy, heartbreak, family dysfunction—all of these emotional issues can lead to destructive behavior that causes you to be a bad parent and therefore causes your child to have problems. After all, hating the other parent is like drinking poison and hoping someone else gets sick. These stories show a variety of issues.

I loved him/her more than anyone I have ever met. We were soul mates. I adored her/him. I wanted us to spend every waking moment together. Making love was the best ever. Having a child together was perfect. Breaking up absolutely broke my heart. I am devastated. I have been depressed since the separation. I'll never get over the heartbreak. I still want to get back together. I cannot function.

***

We have two precious little children, but now I find out the last child is not mine. I have been taking care of that child for three years. It tears me up to think that someone else is that little guy's father. Now, I see her and am around both kids when I go pick up my child. I just can't get over the resentment I have over having been used for so long. Worse, the way I discovered this was from the kids when they told me that they had another dad. I want custody just to spite her. She made a fool of me.

***

Everything my sister does is perfect. Everything I do is flawed. So, now I have this precious baby, but the circumstances are not what my family hoped for. Again my sister will outshine me.

***

I'm Jewish and he is Baptist. This is going to get interesting.

***

My family has a big reunion every July fourth. It is the only time we all get together and it is always at a big resort or the beach. It is always out of state, but she says I can't take our child to another state. Is that right?

***

I live in my apartment and she lives in her apartment. We have never been to court for anything. I signed the birth certificate at the hospital. Her parents' insurance covered it. I take stuff over for the baby. We seemed to be working things out without any rules. However, now she talks about going back to nursing school and taking the baby to live with her parents who live two hundred miles away while she is in school. They say I will have to pay them child support or pay for private pre-school tuition. They also go to a church that only worships on Saturdays. They say that I can't have visits on Saturday because it will mess up their church day. Did I mention they don't believe in celebrating holidays?

***

These are just some sample issues. You might be a lot better off than these people. Time to get back out your paper and pencil, computer, or tablet and answer some more questions. You know the drill. (These questions, along with answer space are at Appendix C, "Your Issues" for you to hand write, or at www.singleparentreferee.com.)

Here are the questions to help you figure out what **your** issues are:

1. List your issues with the other parent. Write down what hurts or angers you the most.

2. What religious faith will this child follow? What are your options? What and why? Who does it matter to the most?

3. What school/daycare will this child attend? Who deals with the teachers? Which parent will the school call first? Can you afford a private school? Is there a family tradition anywhere? Does it matter? Are there issues?

4. What values do we have that are different from the other parent? (This could take pages!)

5. What role will grandparents play, and can you depend on them to play fair?

The third step: Let's get just the facts.

You've heard the old expression, plan for the best, but prepare for the worst. Good advice for any parent. But you can't plan or prepare without facts to guide you. This step is all about gathering facts, or information, about your family. You need to organize all of your information, and as you do that, don't act like you are going to court, but THINK like you might have to go to court as a last resort. You need to get all of the information about both of you along with all family members together and available. It is important to get all of this information early and keep it updated. Get a calendar that you keep for every year. Mark significant things that happen on any given date in the calendar. Use the calendar like a diary, and put it where you can find it easily. (At www.singleparentreferee.com there is a calendar you can print off.)

It is a lot of work to assemble the information we ask of you, but it is critically important. Why? If you do have to go to court to seek custody or visitation with your child or to handle a dispute with your child's school or doctor, this information will be your greatest strength. Write it down now and update it regularly. In five years, this information could be a lifesaver. Remember, if you don't already have the information put together, later it will be much harder to get together.

Trust me, over the eighteen years of raising a child, there is a strong possibility you will face conflict or need this information. You may need it for mediation, visitation, custody or child support hearings. Some of the information is basic. Of course you know your child's name, however you may forget the full names of step-siblings who are older. You may forget medical issues or school names. You will for certain forget school names if there were three different schools in the first grade. Write it down now and put it in a safe place. Once again, in five years if there is a dispute, this information will be gold.

Before we get started, go to your kids' and other parents' social networks, i.e. Facebook/LinkedIn/Twitter, etc. Print a copy of the pages that have important information or down right trash. Click "save." Just put it in your file. It is amazing what you will learn. Look at your own page (or the page of the parent you are helping or counseling). Make sure everyone in your house has cleaned up their stuff. "I like to raise hell and smoke dope" is not a good quote on Facebook for a parent who might want custody of their kid. "Who's coming to my party this Saturday night?" That's information you might want to have when your teenager is visiting the other parent who happens to be working this Saturday night.

Never, ever forget that text messages, internet postings, email messages and blogs can all get you into huge trouble. Serious trouble. If it can be printed off and is not protected, it can be used against you. By the way, don't tell anyone your passwords.

You will begin by including the names and significant information regarding everyone in the picture, especially other children who may not be part of this drama. Include your other children who may be grown and other children you have from other relationships. By showing your good track record with regard to raising your other children, you are providing the best evidence of your parenting skills. Lookout, you might have other kids who have been in trouble or have had serious problems. Don't hide that but be ready to explain it. That situation might be very different. The reason for this kid's problems may have something to do with your ex. What is the other parent's track record?

Plan for the best and prepare for the worst. In other words, plan your journey but bring along a jack and spare tire. Hopefully, your relationships with the other parent and grandparents, aunts and uncles will be helpful, loving and encouraging. If they are not, then information is the key to success. Get the information while you can. In ten years no one will remember the facts unless you have documented them now. In ten years your child could be in the teenage years when lots of things can change. In ten years you may not have access to social security numbers, old addresses, bank statements, schools and teachers' names. Be sure you get this information legally.

- **REFEREE'S RULE:** Try to avoid a court battle unless your child is at risk. Then go to court fully prepared.

- **PRACTICAL TIP:** Keep your notes in a safe place and never give out your www.singleparentreferee.com password.

- **TALKING TIP:** "Things are not going well. Would you go with me to counseling or mediation? I think we can make parenting work better together."

- **LEGAL TIP:** If you think you are going to have a custody or visitation fight, hire a good attorney. Start asking around about which lawyers in your town handle these cases. Don't hire out of the phone book or off a bus sign. Get references. When and how to hire a lawyer is at Chapter Five.

When my ex and I got together, my daughter was ten years old and I had custody of her. My ex was so manipulative of her, she began rebelling at age thirteen. Her problems were directly related to my ex's controlling, mean behavior. When we separated and I was able to raise my daughter alone, my daughter became a wonderful, productive, successful young woman. Now I see the same pattern with my younger child by this ex. My ex is playing the same mind-games and using the same control stuff which leads to anger and rebellion.

***

This is a great example of how information can help. When the ex describes the problems you used to have with your older daughter, it is important to know all of that cleared up when you got your daughter away from your ex. The track record a parent has with other kids is always important. It can be used for or against you. How can the rebellion with the previous child be traced to the ex? It can if you have taken time to assemble good information. (These questions along with answer space are in Appendix D, "Just the Facts" for you to answer or at www.singleparentreferee.com.)

- **REFEREE'S RULE**: You might be a grandparent and find yourself documenting irresponsible behavior of your own child regarding your grandchild. Keep it confidential. Pray you won't need to use it, but take care of your grandchild first over an irresponsible parent. Plan ahead as a grandparent.

1. List names, schools, jobs, housing.

- Write down full names and detailed information about each child, the other parent, any significant stepparent or other ex and their children. This even includes custody information about the other parent's other children. It may surprise you this information is important, but an ex-stepparent can be very significant. What conflict did the prior spouse/lover have before you? At some point this could be very important information. As for the other parent's children, it's important to know if your ex has lost custody of children before. Does another parent or grandparent have this child or other children of that parent most of the time? That makes a difference.

- You need to get detailed school and daycare information about each child. Why does this matter? Perhaps the years the child lived with you/your family, his grades were good and he excelled in music or sports. Then, when the child lived with the other family, his grades slipped and he got in trouble all of the time. That matters. You need the information (grades, teacher reports) that backs you up.

- You need not only information about your current job, but also about your previous jobs. You'll need information about the other parent's jobs, too. Frequent job loss can show that person to be difficult, irresponsible and not financially stable. But you have to list all the jobs to prove the point. The work information can also show the person to be so successful he or she keeps getting promoted and sought out by better and better employers.

- You need the name of a character witness at your current job. This is someone who can verify you have a good boss who understands your parental issues and who knows you are responsible for both school and health care. This could one day affect custody and child support.

- You need detailed information about where you live, the neighborhood and who lives there along with the same information about the other parent. Living in one place shows stability, responsibility and permanency. Knowing your neighbors is positive. It is not a good thing to not know anyone on your street. Consider this:

My next door neighbor has been my baby-sitter and has helped me when I have needed my child picked up from school. She has helped when I have had car trouble. She brought over food when my brother passed away. She is listed as the emergency person at the school if they cannot reach me.

***

Mr. H., who is my supervisor, has seen me be the parent on call for my child when any problem occurred at school. He knows I have left work to take my child to the doctor and that I provide the health insurance through my job. He has seen me bring my child to work on snow days when school was canceled. My boss has helped sponsor my child's baseball team when I was coaching and we needed business sponsors. He knows my ex was never available for emergencies. His phone number is: X

***

My ex gets fired from every job because she gets into arguments with other employees and can't show up on time. There have been at least four jobs in the last eighteen months.

***

My grown sister also lives with us. She is going to college part-time and picks up the kids from school most days.

***

We live in the house with my mother because we help her pay utilities and she helps supervise the kids' homework since she is a retired school teacher.

***

My brother lives with us because he just got out of prison and can't find a job, so he hangs around the house and runs errands for me and a fellow down the street. (Kick the brother out and rewrite that story.)

***

Facts like these will also hurt or help your case, depending on which side you are on:

My ex's forty-year-old brother is bipolar and has been evicted from previous apartments because of fights with the neighbors. My ex lets him live with her because she takes his social security disability check.

***

2. List medical history.

You'll also need detailed health insurance and medical information on yourself, your children, the other parent, and others. Beware of the Health Insurance Portability and Accountability Act (HIPAA), health information privacy federal laws that make it difficult to get those records. Make sure you do not violate those laws. In general,

30

you are entitled to medical records on yourself and your children, but you need a court order to get anyone else's, UNLESS they give it to you or leave it out for you to see. That is why it is important to permanently save and store this information when you have proper access to it.

If you work in a medical facility, you could lose your job if you get medical records without proper permission. Do not ask your friends to get this information for you. It is a violation of the law. Same with banking information. It is a crime to obtain this information by illegally getting into the banking systems. Just collect what you have access to around the house. It is amazing what people leave unprotected and available. Save it when you already have it. Take a picture of it.

Let's consider what you are looking for. What information might you need?

Not useful:
"She got sick a lot."
"Daddy, I have a toothache."

Potentially useful:
"I took her to the Women's Clinic on Vine Avenue for an abortion when she found out she was pregnant by a man whose name she could not remember. Here is the canceled check and records she left in my car."

"He left his credit card receipts at my house which showed he went to the emergency room for an accident." These stories show a problem:

> *"Daddy, I was in the hospital because my tooth abscessed when mom wouldn't take me to the dentist." (Make sure the dental insurance was in place and the dental bills paid.)*

***

> *She was in a car accident which led to chronic back pain. She started taking pain medication and now takes a lot of different*

prescription drugs. Often, the kids stay with me because she is so out of it. They are always late to school when they stay with her.

***

Sickle cell runs in my family, but nobody has had the trait in my generation until now. My family knows the consequences and symptoms of sickle cell disease. We understand the best treatment for our child who has sickle cell.

***

3. List mental health history.

You will also be outlining mental health history. This family history is different than medical history and much more sensitive. First, identify the mental health issues. Second, try to list what triggers problems. Third, what can be done to avoid the problems? As the story below demonstrates, documenting with specific information will help you decide if you need to take action to get custody of your child. You must not leave your child in a dangerous situation!

Her new husband has a serious anger management problem. He goes off at the least little thing. My child says she never knows what will trigger a big scene. He gets angry at my ex a lot over really stupid things. When he can't find the channel changer for the TV, he makes everyone in the house get up and clean while he yells and screams. He has been arrested for domestic violence before.

***

A critical element of mental health history is substance abuse. Addiction problems, alcohol, pills and illegal drugs impact your kids. Doing nothing about these problems will lead to a crisis. Doing something may require a confrontation to help get this under control. Help from other family members and help from professionals is the first step.

This is just as true when the problem is YOU. This story tells it:

> *We were both smoking a lot of weed when we were first together. She graduated to cocaine after the baby was born. It's a miracle the kid didn't test positive at birth. I was holding my breath. Then she got straight until we broke up. I cleaned up because my job drug-tested me every month. She got worse. Her parents got her into a program. I avoided them because they blamed me for everything. Really she was wilder than I was, but they'll never believe that.*

***

In a situation like this, you must recognize your own strengths and weaknesses and identify his/her family's problems with you. Discuss with your lawyer how you might be able to put parenting time/visitation into a structure so other people can't manipulate visitation because they are mad at you.

4. List criminal history.

Criminal behavior must be addressed because it can cause so much damage to children and adults. Maybe your child needs to be going to the grandparents' or other relatives' homes instead of the home of a parent who mistreats them or engages in drug use or other criminal behavior when the child is around. Sometimes it is your child or another child in the household who has a criminal history or may be headed in that direction. Getting the facts down may help you see what you need to do. It is easy to find out who has been arrested and for what. Consider these stories, then search the internet.

> *As a teenager she had assault charges against her for fights at school and home. Then she had an old boyfriend who had a restraining order against her due to domestic assault. Her police record reads like a trash novel. Every time I go to get my child she tries to start something. I can tell she is trying to push my buttons so I'm the one who will be arrested.*

***

The internet police records in our county show he was convicted for simple (drug) possession while he was a student at a university in Washington. Then in Portland, Oregon, he pled guilty to misdemeanor possession with intent to sell. A year later in San Francisco, he was pulled over in a stolen van and his co-defendants all pled guilty to drug charges, but he went to trial and got it dismissed. However, something else happened in Arizona just last year involving drugs. What? How do I find out?

***

5. List non-criminal legal history.

Listing non-criminal problems like bankruptcy, divorces and paternity, especially any DNA testing turns up really interesting stuff. In the story below, that parent might have problems, may be irresponsible or may just be down on his or her luck. Whatever the reason, these issues affect your child.

My ex has had four different DNA tests done by four different women who thought he was their baby's daddy. Then he filed bankruptcy two times to avoid jail for child support. I think his other petition for custody just got settled!

***

6. List significant dates.

The dates that matter include wedding dates, separation dates, moving dates. You may have already listed many of them in the above categories. The details can prove you are able to be objective about irresponsible behavior or show there is real instability that threatens your kids. Stories like these are rare, but they happen.

She introduced the kids to her first "fiancé" on February 14, 2007, then on May 31, 2007 she brought home someone else and introduced him as a "fiancé." Then over Thanksgiving of

*the same year, she took some guy named Bill to her parents'
house for Thanksgiving dinner. To everyone's shock, she made
a surprise announcement that Bill would be our kids "new
daddy." The kids were really upset with the "new daddy" part.*

***

*He left us on January 1, 2008 and quit paying rent and utilities.
We had to move in with my parents on March 1, 2008,which is
also when I put the kids into their new school. He got married
on January 2, 2008 and took a cruise from January 2 to
January 8.*

***

7. List crisis events.

Anything from a car accident to a hurricane to a death in the family
can place enormous stress on children. You need the details. They
can show, as in the first story below, you are good at making a bad
situation better with your helpful and responsible behavior.

*Her car got rear-ended at a red light and an ambulance took
everyone to the emergency room. She was cut up badly. The
kids freaked out over the blood. I was there immediately with
the insurance card and took the kids home until she could get
better.*

***

*We were all in New Orleans visiting Aunt Mae when Hurricane
Katrina hit. We couldn't get out of the city and stayed in that
God-forsaken arena for five days. We ran out of food and were
terrified by the crime and chaos. I know the kids were
traumatized. It wasn't anybody's fault, but she still blames me.*

***

8. List military issues.

If someone in the family is in the military and away on active duty, this can impact the kids.

- **LEGAL TIP:** Active duty military parents have an entirely different category of rights and protections. An excellent military link is http://usmilitary.about.com/cs/genfamily/a/familycare.htm

My uncle helps as a role model for our sons. When he was overseas with the military, it was hard for the boys.

***

Their dad is in the military and hasn't seen the kids in seven years. They wouldn't know him if he walked in the door alone.
***

We met when we were both in the military and she didn't tell me she was pregnant until after she had been transferred out of the country. She used the military to avoid me and prevent me from contact with my child.

***

The fourth step: Getting it all together

You have decided what you want, you have outlined your issues and you have gathered together the critical information you might need if you ever go to court or face other challenges. Most important, you have thought through some of the things you could face in the future. Now it's time to put all of that together and start the important (and hardest) work on the most important element of this journey: *You.*

This is where you work on your weaknesses. You are the project. Not your child, not your ex and not your family. The main areas are taking care of your health, taking care of your mental health, getting or keeping a stable job, maintaining stable housing and surrounding yourself with good friends. (Yes, that means it's time to dump the bad friends.)

Getting yourself together starts with a goal and a plan. If you have anger or resentment, then live by the motto "The best revenge is living well." Resolve you will get or stay in good physical shape. Exercise and work out. Do not smoke anything. Take vitamins and not pain killers. If you have depression, obtain professional counseling. Get on a super-healthy diet to get yourself "living well." Always try to look your best. You can do that and still shop at thrift stores. Call it "adventure shopping."

Work at getting stress under control so you will look and feel more confident. Make a time-line for getting your job and housing where you want them to be. This might take several years, but have a realistic plan and mark your progress.

Don't have more babies until you know you are in a positive, permanent relationship with Mister or Ms. Right. This should be someone you marry. He or she is out there. Wait for the right one and don't settle for less. Make sure you are protected in case you have sex. Don't get a disease.

Now, dump the bad friends. You know who they are. These are the people who always lead you astray. They never do positive things. And trouble is always around when they show up. Move if you must, but get away from bad influences.

- **REFEREE'S RULE:** The best revenge is living well.

- **PRACTICAL TIP:** Get a workout buddy.

- **TALKING TIP:** ''Yes, I can.''

- **LEGAL TIP:** Stay away from friends who attract cops.

CHAPTER THREE

What to Do About the Problems:
The Single Parent Referee's Top Ten Roadblocks

Life is full of roadblocks that can get in your way and can stop positive, forward movement in its tracks. To raise a great kid when you and the other parent are not together, you must first spot those roadblocks, learn how to deal with them, then decide if you should hit them straight on or steer around them. It takes wisdom and patience to make the right choice. Sometimes the right choice is to take no action at all. If something is already working well, just wait and watch. Once you choose your approach, it takes self-control and patience to stick with it in a calm, "just the facts" manner. Think of yourself as a driver, identifying the best lane for you and learning to stay in your own lane no matter what the roadblocks of life bring you. Stay in your lane.

Of course, it would be easy if things were as simple as one person driving in one lane. Unfortunately, when you add the other parent, the children, the grandparents and others it can seem like you are negotiating a crazy, ten-lane highway with people in the other lanes trying to run you off the road. Do not let the folks in the other lane get to you! Use your self-control to stay in your own lane.

The top ten areas where roadblocks exist are:

1. **Communication. We just can't talk.**
2. **Family. They don't help but meddle.**
3. **The Significant Other. This get's really tricky.**
4. **Bullies. Other kids are mistreating my child.**
5. **Safety. Pools, pot and pistols.**
6. **Childcare. Who are these people?**
7. **Rules. They are different at each house.**

8. **Parenting Time/Visitation. It is a power struggle.**
9. **Issues. My child has school problems and/or emotional problems.**
10. **Money. There is never enough.**

1. Communication. We just can't talk.

You shouldn't be surprised that communication is the most common and serious roadblock. After all, if the two of you could talk to each other, maybe you would not have broken up. It's not just what is said and not said, but also what is understood and misunderstood. Then, there's the reaction and over-reaction. Communication problems are usually a reflection of the real problem, which might be money, heartbreak, infidelity, abuse or something else.

Communication problems fall into these categories:
   A. The Rant and Verbal Abuse –One or both parties are ugly, abusive and sarcastic.

   B. The Freeze Out – No one talks at all. Silence.

   C. The Liar – Someone cannot tell the truth.

A. The Rant and the Verbal Abuse

I can't get my son's mother to talk about important stuff without going off about something. I called her yesterday to talk about Danny's school problems. He has three D's and two F's. Instead of talking about what to do, all she could do was to yell at me: "I TOLD you that private school was a bad idea and would be too hard for him. You insisted he go there because your family has always gone there, but you don't care if it's good for Danny." She cusses at me every time we talk.

***

It's no surprise that the rant and the verbal abuse are the communication problems in that story.

When one or two parents cannot talk to each other without things always turning ugly, they must find alternative ways to communicate. Text-messaging is best for short, quick messages confirming instructions or short information. For example: "Teacher-parent meeting 2:30 tomorrow." E-mail is better than texting for longer, informative messages (for example, a summary of what happened at the teacher-parent meeting, or an explanation of the child's medication).

While e-mail and texting are the best ways to communicate when one or both parents can't talk in a civilized manner, there are some important things to remember. Namely, e-mails and texts can be saved and used against you in court and elsewhere. So don't curse, threaten or talk bad. That works both ways. You need to take care of YOUR own interests by saving e-mails and texts you get from your ex, because you might need them as evidence for your side in court or elsewhere. Have a system for saving e-mails and text messages to a file you can access later.

Whether you communicate verbally or electronically, it is critical that you never talk bad to the other parent or about the other parent in front of your child. That is not easy sometimes, but you must follow that rule. Stay in your lane with your communication.

Another strategy is to find a third party, such as a grandparent or aunt, who will be the go-between, then use that person to help you communicate. Refuse to participate in verbal abuse, verbal ranting or freezing out the other parent. Instead, ask your go-between to tell the other parent in the future you will be communicating with him or her only by e-mail and texting. When a real need for extra contact arises, ask this third party to help communicate important information.

- **REFEREE'S RULE:** It takes two to argue. Do not respond to arguments.

- **PRACTICAL TIP:** Lower your expectations. Things don't change overnight.

- **TALKING TIP:** Silence is golden.

- **LEGAL TIP:** Text messages and voice messages that are ugly and abusive are very helpful/hurtful/**useful** in court. Save them.

B. The Freeze-out

Total silence can drive a parent crazy. It's a short trip. Have you found your third person who will agree to be your go-between yet? To deal with the freeze-out, you *must* find that third person. Otherwise *you* will be the parent who is ranting and screaming.

Would his or her sister or mother or aunt agree to this job? This third person can eventually be your ally, so be careful that you don't take advantage of them or expect them to be your counselor. Find a person whom you both trust. Someone whom the other parent trusts the most is even better. For instance, if the other side's sister is your go-between and she sees how reasonable and helpful you are, then she will be the person who tells her sibling to cooperate. She will see you are a good and helpful parent. She might be your best ally. Don't make her mad.

Always follow these rules for the go-between:

- Just the facts are reported. For example, "Our child is in a play this weekend and needs to be back at the school Saturday night at 5 pm." **Stop right there.** Do *not* add: "And, since it is your visitation weekend, that is your responsibility." That is obvious.

- Neither parent reacts negatively to the facts of the go-between. "Thank you for telling me." **Stop right there**. Don't say: "I can't do that, I've gotten tickets for the kid and me to see the Lakers play basketball this Saturday. Nobody told me there was a play." Find out more before you make a choice, then report your choice in a matter–of-fact way.

- The go-between does not become the negotiator or mediator. "I will call our child and find out more about the play." **Stop right there.** Don't say: "What do you think if I tell

her that we are skipping the play? How important is this play?"
- *Never* take your anger out on the messenger. **Stop right there** -- before you speak in anger! The go-between is just the messenger.

Often, being silent in the face of a difficult situation is the best solution, even if it takes all your strength to keep your mouth shut! At other times, silence is absolutely wrong. If your child's parent calls you at three a.m. to tell you your child is in the emergency room with injuries from a bad car wreck, that is no time to be silent. You should be asking how badly the child is hurt and where is the emergency room so you can go check on him or her. Later, when you get there, silence might well be the best policy, especially if your ex is trying to make a bad situation worse by arguing over who's to blame.

C. The Liar

How *do* you cope with a liar? Lying is a major character flaw and an issue serious enough to land the family in court if it gets out of hand. For one thing, lying makes communication difficult because one side never knows what to believe. Worse, one parent might be teaching the child how to lie if that parent says things like, "Don't tell Daddy that Sam stayed over here this weekend."

Always keep in mind a confrontation might take you to court, so be careful what you threaten. Be prepared to follow through. How much lying are you willing to put up with? The little lies? For example when he/she says, "I'm just five minutes away," when really they are at least thirty minutes away, or the big lies, such as: "We have *not* had our power turned off" as they sit in total darkness and have no heat. Or the *really* big lies, such as: "My new husband has *not* been in jail for child pornography," when in fact, he has.

Teaching a child to lie must be dealt with *at once*. When your child is lying to you, or is being taught to lie, counseling is necessary. Court action may also be necessary. It's particularly serious when the child lies compulsively. If that's happening, you absolutely must get the child counseling to change that behavior. Make sure you let your child know that *you* know she/he lies.

2. Family. They don't help but meddle.

Sometimes grandparents or other family members don't help but meddle and cause problems. This can be a tremendous roadblock, particularly when you consider what a huge help cooperative grandparents can be when you are raising a child.

The trouble usually begins when grandparents or other family members form strong opinions about everything you do. They want to impose their values and they want you to do everything their way. Or, they perceive you are to blame for everything wrong in their family. Whatever the reality, they will blame you. It is hard to fight that perception, so the best strategy is to avoid any possible confrontation. This is a classic example of family members getting out of their own lane and into yours.

Often, the root problem is the grandparents didn't approve of the relationship to begin with. Perhaps they were upset over the pregnancy in the beginning, or advised that you break up from the start. This is made worse by the fact that it is easy for young parents to become defensive and hostile when their parenting decisions are questioned. Whether it's your own parents or your ex's parents and family, if they feel this way about you, it is hard to get beyond this slight. Perhaps you believe that they thought you were never good enough for their son or daughter. That creates major insecurity whether it is true or not. Still, you must get over it!

Sometimes the trouble is simply a personality conflict between one or both parents and grandparents, or there may still be bad feelings about ugly things that were said in the past. It gets complicated.

Whatever the reason for the problems, getting past your anger is particularly important when the grandparents are offering something that can benefit your children, such as child care. Don't cut off your nose to spite your face. These may be things you really need help with. How can you get what you need without getting the grandparents/family too involved in your life? Making some ground rules and spelling out the specific things you need from them can help. You might want to write down a set of rules or requests. Calling these "requests" instead of "rules" may keep others from getting defensive.

Remember, grandparents can help most with childcare and some expenses if they are in your corner. Use them to help. Write down when you need childcare and for what. Ask them if they are available for any, but not necessarily all, of these times. It might be best for everyone if you avoid getting too chummy with them. Don't tell them too much about your personal life. Never tell them your secrets.

However, you should also consider whether you *do* have secrets that cause them to be suspicious. Are you involved in something (drugs, alcohol, partying) which gives them reason to disapprove of your lifestyle? Are there accusations by others that major problems such as domestic violence, drug or alcohol abuse or mental health issues are looming on the horizon? Are the grandparents trying to help you avoid disaster or are they pushing you toward a crisis? This is where an objective third person can help you understand which direction you should go.

Conflicts like this can take you in a truly bad direction if you over-react. Ending up in court with family against you is a path you do not want to go down. It is worth keeping your cool and being smart to avoid this scenario.

Another good choice is a confidential church or family counselor, who might be more objective. While this person may not know all of the players, a trained counselor can advise you and help you stay calm and maintain control of your emotions. It may be that the grandparents don't realize just how critical they are or how it feels when you experience their disapproval. The counselor can help to clue them in.

This third party can also give you an honest answer about whether *you* are being too defensive or hostile. Remember, being defensive will only lead to further problems and misunderstandings, so check your attitude.

- **REFEREE'S RULE:** Family can be your best friend one minute and your worst enemy the next.

- **PRACTICAL TIP:** Don't tell everything, even to family.

- **TALKING TIP:** "I really appreciate all of your help. You have been wonderful."

- **LEGAL TIP:** You can also have joint custody with family members. This is where you and that relative file a petition and go to court to ask the judge for joint custody so the other relative can help with child care, school pick up, medical assistance or even health insurance. Both parents must agree to this.

2. The Significant Other. This gets really tricky.

What is your ex's significant other like? That is an important question, given the enormous difference this person can make in your life and the life of your child. If the significant other is wonderful, generous, positive and helpful, then you don't need to read this part of the book. You are very lucky. However, if that is not the case, read on.

If you are not lucky, sometimes your ex's significant other seems like the wicked stepparent or a home-wrecker. Or maybe that person is both. Either way, it can be bad.

Let's start by considering that person's point of view. Being a stepparent or significant other is a very difficult job under the best of circumstances, and usually circumstances are far from perfect. The stepparent has to understand all the personal dynamics of the relationships and be kind and sweet to a child who is not his/hers. When there are other children in the home, they compete for attention, too. Many children say the stepmother or stepfather is always picking on them.

It is a difficult truth that often, no matter what the stepparent does, the child will always feel the stepparent is picking on them. The child will always insist the stepparent is the bad guy. Consider this story:

Jeffery is 12 and gets his feelings hurt easily, perhaps too easily, however, he perceives his stepfather is harsher on him than the stepsiblings. He says when all of the kids tracked mud all over the house, the other kids were sent to the bathroom to wash up, BUT Jeffery says he was whipped. Then, Jeffery was told to clean it all up. I later found out the other kids are less than five years old and as the older kid in charge, Jeffery was specifically asked by his stepfather to keep the muddy kids out of the house.

***

Here is a situation where it is very important to stay in your lane unless your child's safety is at risk. Otherwise, coming into conflict with a stepparent can create serious roadblocks. This means if there is a personality problem with your child and his stepparents and/or stepsiblings, they will have to work it out themselves. Stay out of it unless safety is involved. Working through conflict is a great life lesson for your child.

Most of the time a child (especially a teenager) wants to come home and vent. After they unload their complaints on their parent, they are fine and go away fully consoled and rejuvenated. Often they totally forget what they were even complaining about. However, the parent who received all of this negative raw data about the other parent's household must process it and find a way to decide if this is real, real bad or really nothing at all. Again, stay in your lane. Use wisdom and patience.

Be on your child's side, but get the facts, too. You can still support your child and be a listening parent. Find out what is real by asking your child specific questions. Also, ask other kids who might have seen the situation for their opinions. Keep in mind sometimes your child might be trying to get more attention from the other parent, or might be jealous of the other family in that parent's life. Whatever you do, do not automatically assume the worst about a stepparent unless you see bruises or hear the yelling yourself.

If you do see bruises and hear yelling, that's a different story. Always take action if you know your child has been abused. However, if you suspect child abuse but are not sure, do this: first, take the child to a neutral friend or neighbor, away from where the suspected abuse happened. Then, talk with your child in the

46

presence of your neutral friend about whether this is serious enough to go to the doctor or emergency room to confirm that what you are seeing and hearing is abuse.

This is not a step to take lightly. The reason: When you go to the doctor or emergency room, if they confirm child abuse has occurred, they will call the Department of Children's Services for an investigation. This may result in you or your family filing a court petition for custody of your child.

It is important for your child to know you are defending him or her, and they have someone to turn to in times of real trouble. It is also important for them to see you get all of the facts and get them right before taking any action. That is why you sit down with your child and write down what he or she says happened and then have a calm discussion with the other people involved to find out what really happened. Your children need to know they have an ally in you, but they also need to know they can't make up stuff just because they feel resentment toward their stepparent or their other parent.

So, when should you take action? When your child is visibly upset, crying or emotionally upset, then you listen very carefully to your child. Take written notes about what your child tells you, then read those notes to someone objective. This will help you see if this is more than a minor outburst. Write down how you will talk with the other parent. When you call the other parent, use your notes so you stay in your lane and stick to "just the facts." If you over-react, then you will not have credibility when you really need it.

- **REFEREE'S RULE:** You must take immediate action if you believe your child is being abused physically, mentally or sexually. *You must protect your child when safety is a factor.* If there is abuse, the first step is to take your child to your pediatrician or other treating doctor. Ask the doctor if this is abuse that should be reported to your state's Department of Children's Services.

- **PRACTICAL TIP:** Take notes on everything, especially names and phone numbers of potential witnesses and investigators. The nurse at the emergency room could be your most important contact.

- **TALKING TIP:** Don't talk about this over and over with your child. Let your child heal and get beyond this, even though it might take therapy for both of you.

- **LEGAL TIP:** If the doctor agrees abuse has occurred, then he or she must file a report. This report is what you should use in court when you file a petition to keep your child away from the person who was the abuser. If you think it was the other parent, supervised visits are often the first step, depending upon the extent of the abuse.

- **LEGAL TIP:** Remember, sexual abuse must be reported to state authorities. It is investigated by the state and in most states a Sexual Assault Resource Center is involved in the investigation. The perpetrator will be prosecuted.

Most conflict is not abuse, but misunderstanding. Children often perceive mistreatment from very ordinary situations. Young girls are quick to get their feelings hurt. Consider this story.

Brittany's stepmother left her job early (which could get her in trouble) to get groceries for the weekend (which she paid for out of her own bank account) and to pick Brittany up for her visitation with her dad (he was golfing). When she pulled into the driveway, she announced to both her own daughter and Brittany, "OK, everyone help carry in the groceries," to which Brittany replied, "I don't have to do that. Mom said I am not the maid over here and I don't have to do chores."

***

What action should you take? In the case of Brittany, her stepmom should ask the dad to send an e-mail to Brittany's mother along these lines:

We truly don't want this to be a big deal, but I want to straighten it out so there are no problems in the future. (Explain as above.) What was said is not the issue, however Brittany's perception that she does not have to help at our house is not a good characteristic for her to develop. I want her to always want to help out wherever she is and whomever she is visiting. How do you think we should handle this so it does not cause a misunderstanding?

***

Being calm, objective and using e-mail keeps this from becoming another communication battle between the dad and the mom.

If, in this example, the stepmom made Brittany carry in all the groceries herself, then start dinner while the stepmom and her own daughter watched television, that's different. The mom should write an e-mail to all, giving these and other specific examples and asking if there was bad behavior on Brittany's part that led to the harsher treatment. Clearly address this as unfair treatment, but encourage Brittany to be helpful at all times.

Whatever you do, stay calm and keep your emotions in check. Yelling will not help your child get along better with stepparents. Stick to the facts, use e-mail and try to understand the stepparent's point of view.

If the significant other is the person your beloved abandoned you for, then this is a very difficult situation to deal with. How are you supposed to graciously share your child with the person who ruined your life? How are you supposed to cheerfully welcome into your world the person who torpedoed everything you cherish? To the parent who was left behind, accepting the home-wrecker feels so wrong on so many levels. It is insulting, demeaning, immoral, disrespectful and painfully impossible. Thus, you have to **fake it.**

When your beloved chooses to leave and take up a life with another, that is not your child's fault, nor is it something that should burden your child. As much as you might despise and detest the home-wrecker, if the other parent lives with and/or marries that person, your child will visit their home and have a relationship with him or her.

49

Unfortunately, as a responsible parent, you have no choice but to have contact with this person. You have to fake it with the best acting skills you can muster, and always stay in character before your child. You have to tell a child the other parent loves him or her. You must never speak badly of the other parent or the home-wrecker in front of your child, even if it kills you. Chapter Seven will help you with faking it.

The hardest part may be to keep your mouth shut. If your child hears you trash the other parent and/or talk bad about the significant other, the consequences are huge. Your child will:

- Feel insecure about both of you and be emotionally torn.

- Hide how he/she feels about that other parent.

- Hide what goes on at the other house.

- Learn to exclude you from events that include the other parent.

- Sneak around about doing things with the other parent.

- Manipulate you both, especially if the child is a teenager.

- Tell the other parent and make matters worse.

- **REFEREE'S RULE:** It takes two to fight, or in this case, three. Do not participate in arguments with the stepparent or significant other.

- **PRACTICAL TIP:** Fake being nice even if it kills you.

- **TALKING TIP:** Silence is more golden than ever here. What you tell your kids about the stepparent is likely to be repeated.

- **LEGAL TIP:** Joint custody with a stepparent is possible, but can have dangerous and serious consequences. Get legal advice for that.

4. Bullies. And other challenges of dealing with people.
Children often feel the same way about stepsiblings, or cousins as they do about stepparents. It is perceived that they are always picking on your child. Being in the other parent's house with older stepsiblings can create rivalry that even the best parent cannot easily diffuse. However, while kids often fuss and fight, it's a different story if these children bully or mistreat your child. Since you don't actually see this behavior, sometimes it is hard to tell if there's a real problem or routine sibling disagreement.

How can you tell the difference? Start by sitting down with your child and writing down the things he or she reports. Then read it aloud to your child, and see how it sounds. Does it sound like, "He looked at me funny," or "She changed the channel when I was watching TV?" When you read it aloud, it's often easy to tell if it's typical kid stuff. But, what about these descriptions: "When Daddy was gone, they locked me in a closet and tied me up." Or "The older kids put me in the trunk of the car." Or "She always says I'm an idiot and smell like rotten eggs." Consider this scene:

> *When I walk in their house, my stepsister always says, "The freak of nature is here again."*

***

Give the other parent a break on the little things. Siblings always fuss with each other. However, if you and your child believe the behavior rises to the level of bullying, then you must talk to the other parent. Again, e-mail is the best way, so you don't risk a verbal argument. It is very important that you stick just to the facts as you know them, and point out any bruises your child blames on the stepsibling in question. Be factual and careful not to sound like you are blaming, accusing or criticizing. Stick to the facts.

Here's an example of what you might say in your e-mail to the other parent, not the stepparent:

> *I know kids might fuss and fight, just acting like kids, but I want to help our child be happier with you. He says he feels bullied, but I don't know whether that is a one-time silly fuss,*

or a real, on-going issue. If you could take him out for ice cream or someplace where just the two of you could talk, then you can find out if this bullying he talks about is real or just something he likes to complain about. That way, you will know if you need to help him deal with this, ignore this or work it out. I also know sometimes kids just like to complain. What do you think?

The bottom line: even if what your child experiences at the other parent's house is minimal, both parents must still acknowledge and deal with the way he or she feels about it. For the child, the lesson to be learned here may be how to deal with people of all ages.

REFEREE'S RULE: Don't over-react to perceived bullying, but never ignore it.

PRACTICAL TIP: Take a karate class with your child.

TALKING TIP: "Tell me, again, exactly what happened to you."

LEGAL TIP: Always report to the school, both in person and in writing, when you believe your child is being bullied at school. Copy the board of education. Most schools are developing zero tolerance policy for bullying.

5. Safety. Pistols, pools and pot.

Do you feel your child is in danger at the other parent's house? Do you have basic safety concerns? Do other people say you are worrying too much? Do you have any basis for your worries? How do you stay in your own lane on safety issues?

What if there are guns at the other house, or your two-year-old can't swim and the other parent's apartment complex has a pool? How do you handle it when the other parent does not share your concerns about basic safety? This is one time when responding carefully and effectively could be a matter of life and death. These stories are real.

The swimming pool is unattended and not fenced. Our child is only two years old and cannot swim. The child's mother says not to worry, but she is always distracted by her home business and other kids. The news reports kids drowning all the time, so I can't help but worry.

***

Her husband is a police officer and he always takes his gun belt off and leaves it on the dining room table where the kids walk through and see it and touch it. I've seen their friends come by and hold it.

***

Drugs have always been a part of his lifestyle. When we were together, he smoked pot regularly. Last month he got fired for flunking a drug screen. Now, our daughter keeps telling me there are times when she can't wake him in the morning. What if there is an emergency and she can't wake him? Is he doing drugs when she is over there?

***

Start by assuming the other parent is equally concerned about safety. *Be very careful here.* Avoid making the other parent feel defensive. Avoid making yourself look paranoid. If you are too uptight, no one will listen to you when you have a real safety concern.

Your first move should be to speak with the other parent and go over each and every safety concern. Stick to the facts, show your intense concern, but don't lose your temper. Talk to the grandparents, too, no matter what type of relationship you have with them. After all, it is their grandchild who is at risk. See if they can help with safety training and being alert about safety.

Basic safety might require you both to take a parenting safety course. That's right, both of you. If you go too, the other parent won't feel like you are putting all the blame on him or her and will be more likely to go along with your suggestion.

- **REFEREE'S RULE:** Safety trumps everything.

- **PRACTICAL TIP:** Teach your child to swim and how to call 911 as early as possible.

- **TALKING TIP:** "I'm going to a parent safety course. Would you go, too?"

- **LEGAL TIP:** Abuse or neglect should be confirmed by a doctor and investigated by your state's Department of Children's Services. It can result in a change of custody.

Involve your kids in safety from an early age. Teach them to stay away from guns and to never let another child touch a gun. Teach your child how to dial 911 early. Find swimming lessons for your child as early as possible. If they are older, don't delay educating them about the dangers of drug abuse. This leads directly to the next major roadblock.

6. Childcare. Who are these people?

So you want the other parent to help out with childcare, but then you have no idea who is keeping your child. Find out who is supervising your kids when they are with the other parent. Ask questions. Is the other parent taking them somewhere inappropriate for their age? Who else is going to be there? Make sure the other parent knows you are paying attention and will take steps to protect your child.

When the child is left with a stranger, this is usually a baby-sitting/childcare issue. Does this person have childcare experience and training? Is this someone your child can get to know for future babysitting? Perhaps the other parent is trying out a new babysitter. On the other hand, maybe the parent dropped the child off with a random neighbor when a last-minute date came up.

Think very carefully before you object to the other parent's babysitting arrangement. Consider whether the child was left with a stranger or a new sitter and if it happens all the time. Try to meet this person, especially if he or she is going to watch your children in the future. Maybe this person is an excellent babysitter, but you just haven't had a chance to meet him or her. Still, keep your eyes open for clues as to whether you can trust this person with your child's safety or not.

Say something like: "I would like for us to use the same babysitter when possible so our child feels comfortable having the same person. Here is the phone number of the lady I use. Could I also call the person you use?"

Before you object, ask yourself honestly: When the other parent is not home or not with your child, do you want to be the back-up sitter? Is anyone in your family available to be the back-up baby-sitter? Could this result in the other parent dumping the child on you when he or she is supposed to have visitation? How would you feel about that? Does the other parent have to be at work during his or her visitation? Can you be flexible, depending on the other parent's work schedule? Could this be a time to make peace with the grandparents so you can enlist their help?

First, decide what you want. If you and your family always want to be the babysitter when the other parent is not with your child, you need to ask for that. Be prepared to have that in a court order if necessary. Chapter Eleven on parenting time has more information on this.

If the other parent works during the time he or she has visitation, there must be safe and appropriate childcare. An eleven-year-old stepsibling as an all-day baby sitter for a younger child is not appropriate. You are entitled to know what the other parent's child-care plan is and who, what and where the daycare is. Often the problem arises when a sudden snow day occurs, or a child is sick and both parents must work.

Get a plan. Talk to other relatives and know ahead of time who can help out in an emergency. Know the other parent's family well enough to know who to call. It's worth developing a relationship so you can have reliable care in a crisis.

- **REFEREE'S RULE:** Children under eleven should not stay home alone.

- **PRACTICAL TIP:** Have an emergency babysitter already lined up whom you can call in a crisis or on a snow day.

- **TALKING TIP:** "Before you hire a babysitter, please call me or my mom and see if we are available."

- **LEGAL TIP:** Leaving a child under eleven years old home alone can result in the child going into state custody and charges against the parent for neglect.

7. Rules. Different parents have different rules.

Any family counselor can tell you if both parents don't communicate, agree upon the rules and enforce them, their kids won't take the parents seriously or follow their rules. They will run all over those parents. That goes double for teenagers.

It is really challenging when there are two parents with two different households that have two different sets of rules. When parents have different rules, they also have different expectations. This can lead to different consequences and different behavior on the part of the child at the two houses. For example, if one household requires a five-year-old to be in bed at eight pm and the other household has a bedtime of ten pm, then the child will be tired after a night at one home and resist going to bed early at the other home. If a teenager has a ten pm curfew at one home but has to be home by midnight at the other home, this, too, will lead to conflict.

Of course, there are always going to be differences, such as donuts for breakfast at one house, eggs and fruit at the other. No one would expect parents who don't live together to do everything the same way. Many habits are just different, not wrong, and it is a matter of both parents being tolerant of differences, as long as they don't threaten the child's safety. Donuts for breakfast may not be the best choice for growing children. But donuts won't poison them, unless the child is a diabetic. Then you are dealing with a safety issue on a different level.

It is wise to choose your battles when it comes to the rules. Write down your rules and take a look at them. Which rules are the same as the rules at the other household? Which are different? Look at the ones that don't fit your life. Are there some you can live with, even if you always have to reinforce your own rules when the kids come back from the other household? Which ones cause the most conflict and trouble among your children? Which might threaten your children's safety and well-being?

Limit your battles to the rules you feel are causing problems and therefore must be enforced in the other home. When you are ready to sit down and negotiate the rules, you may want to use e-mail, or ask the other parent to meet you in a neutral place, such as a coffee shop. Take your list and read from your notes. Make it clear you are not asking the other parent to enforce every teeny, tiny rule you have, just the most important ones. Ask the other parent if there are any rules he or she thinks need to be made or enforced better. Give the other parent a chance to talk and listen without interrupting. This might also be better handled by e-mail. Get the child involved in the list. Your child should know what is being discussed and why, and should help decide the consequences for breaking the rules. For instance, not being ready to leave for school on time can lead to no television/video game/computer time. Next comes the hard part. Enforce the consequences. Every time. Exactly the way you said you would.

- **REFEREE'S RULE:** Consequences should be reasonably related to the actions.

- **PRACTICAL TIP:** Tell your child what the rules are in advance.

- **TALKING TIP:** "You know the consequences, so now it is your choice. If you bite your sister again, you will have chosen to go to bed without any dinner."

- **LEGAL TIP:** Losing your temper with a child can lead to abuse. Excessive discipline is a crime prosecuted by attorneys general in most states.

8. Parenting Time/Visitation. It is a power struggle.

An entire chapter is dedicated to this, along with some workbook space. This has made the top ten list because the power struggle issues are so strong. You will learn more about parenting time/visitation and the issues involved in Chapter Eleven.

When the other parent won't show up on time to pick up the child, shows up unexpectedly or doesn't have your child ready when you come to pick him/her up, this is not about visitation. This is all about control. This is the opportunity each parent has to yank the other parent around and prove just who is really in control.

It might appear to be miscommunication or disorganization when that parent doesn't follow the plan or stay on schedule. After all, sometimes the parent really does experience traffic delays or has to work late (in which case, they should call the other parent in advance). Most of the time, however, it means this parent wants to visit on their terms and is refusing to be controlled by the expectations of the child or the custody agreement. This is about power and who controls whom. Having said that, don't make this World War III just because you have good reason to do so as a result of the other parent's behavior.

To deal with a parent who is always late, send that person an e-mail in plenty of time for them to get it, saying you will wait for fifteen minutes, but you will leave after that because you have things to do. Tell the parent if work is going to cause a delay, then you will agree to a different pick-up time. After fifteen minutes, put a note on the door and go about your business. Take the child with you.

Another strategy is to act as if it is not a big deal. Don't make plans for that night. Don't get stressed. When he or she shows up, she shows up. You don't care. Have neighbor friends over so your child won't even notice the other parent is late because there is so much going on at your house. If your ex's late arrival doesn't appear to upset anyone, maybe he or she won't find satisfaction in being late as a way to demonstrate control. No big deal. No sweat. No cares. No control.

When the other parent shows up late all the time, the rules need to be redrawn to specify time, place and plan. Schedule a time to meet at a neutral, public location such as a coffee shop (never in the home environment). Discuss the schedule and the plan to make sure the other parent understands what it is. Then, ask if it needs to be changed and what will work for everyone's schedule. This discussion could become tense, thus e-mail might be the best way to handle it.

If you use e-mail, say something like: "Sam looks forward to seeing you every other Friday. He is always packed and waiting. We need to set a time for pick up that is more convenient for all of us. The six pm pick up seems to be too early. What would fit your schedule, six-thirty or seven pm?"

If the other parent says seven pm is fine, answer like this: "Okay, seven pm is perfect. He will be ready and waiting at seven sharp. Also, I have a yoga class at seven-fifteen, so I need to leave by five after seven. If for some reason you are late, you will need to come to the gym on Main Street. I'll put him in the child-care room, which will cost ten dollars when you pick him up. Confirm with an e-mail. "

Bottom line, if you have scheduled parenting time/visitation, you better use it. The parent who fails to show up for a scheduled visitation is lower than dirt. There better be a good excuse. The emergency room? The morgue? That's about it. Your child is standing there waiting. The absolute best plan when a parent is unpredictable is to ask a grandparent or relative if you can drop the child off at their house for the visitation. That relative must then deal with the no show parent. Hopefully, the grandparent will be able to either get the other parent to do right or will be a good substitute. It might even enhance the child's time with that side of the family. This story shows the good side:

His sister is a teacher and is very encouraging and positive. She asks our child how her grades are and where she wants to go to college. She has offered to get our daughter into the college prep high school in our city. So, we drop our child at her house where they can spend time together until my ex finally shows up. It is her problem, not mine, if my ex is late.

***

If you are the visiting parent whose child is never ready when you go to pick up, don't require that child to bring an overnight bag or anything else. Avoid the drama of packing the bag. Instead, keep a supply of weekend items such as clothes, toothbrush and toys at your house. Your child will only need shoes and a coat. You might even keep extra shoes with you if leaving the custodial parent's house often requires a long, stressful search for a shoe. If the child is old enough to pack a bag, have a reward for the child if he or she has the backpack ready at the door when you arrive. The best reward is getting a treat together on the way home, a great opportunity to start the visit on a positive note. This story shows how to do it.

> *I pick her up from her mom's, then we call her favorite pizza place and order her favorite pizza, plus some bread sticks. I always tease her and act like we will add anchovies, which she hates. Then, we pick it up together, head home and dig in. It is our special ritual. She usually clips a coupon for us to use. We talk about how much we saved with the coupon and I tell her she is a financial genius for saving so much.*

***

- **REFEREE'S RULE:** Always show up for your visitation and always call or text if you are going to be late. Text a picture of the traffic jam.

- **PRACTICAL TIP:** Don't require an overnight bag for visitation. Keep some things at your place. Plan to do something special your child likes, not just what you like.

- **TALKING TIP:** "What do you want to do at my house this weekend?"

- **LEGAL TIP:** Not returning a child to the parent with custody after a visitation can result in kidnapping charges. Usually, the police are called and with a copy of the court order, the police retrieve the child. That is tremendously stressful for your child, and it doesn't help the erring parent either.

9. Issues. My child has school problems and/or emotional problems.

School problems and emotional problems are two problems that often run together. Serious school problems often involve emotional issues or mental-health issues. Although it's possible the school issue is just one bad teacher or incident with a mean kid, it is often much deeper than that. Similarly, bad grades are sometimes much more significant than bad study habits. Bad conduct in school can be more than class clowning. This story shows a crisis:

> I knew he hated school, but one morning as I was trying to get him out the door he told me he was being recruited by an older kid who was in a gang. He had joined in once and now he was trying to stay out. They were stalking him. He was terrified to go school and he wasn't paying attention in class.

***

This roadblock requires serious attention.

Why? It's not just about you or the other parent. These issues can be serious roadblocks for your child and can literally wreck his or her future. Studies show children who fall behind in the early grades often never catch up, which can block them from success as adults. For this reason, a roadblock that negatively impacts your child's education *must* be removed. Emotional or mental health issues can steer your child into all kinds of trouble. As with school issues, how you respond to mental health issues in the early years makes a huge difference in terms of what path your child follows in the teenage and adult years. These are problems that will not go away without professional help, so you must take the initiative to get this help. Don't waste time placing blame or trying to find fault. Get expert help now.

School or learning problems

Think about what might be causing problems at school. Is your child having trouble learning new concepts and skills? If so, is the teacher doing enough to help? Is your child getting help and support at home? Both homes need a quiet study area. Does your child spend enough time on schoolwork and reading at home? Does your child have attention deficit disorder? Is your child hyperactive or just immature for his or her age (in which case another year could make a big difference)? Does your child have behavior problems that cause him or her to get in trouble at school a lot, or even suspended for bad behavior? Is this a discipline problem or a learning problem? School testing will not cost anything, but sometimes you have to push for it to be done. All schools have someone in charge of testing.

Luckily, your child's school can offer plenty of support, from conferences with your child's teacher to free testing to detect learning disabilities. But *you* must get involved. Sometimes a school counselor will recommend a child be held back, especially in the early years. That is *not* flunking. It is not a bad thing. It just gives your child another year to grow. Some children are slow getting out of the starting gate, but they will be great in the long races of life as long as they are not pushed out too soon.

Are you on the list to speak with the teachers and to meet with the school? If not, get on that list! You cannot find out why, for example, your child is flunking three subjects if you don't talk to the teachers. Make sure you see every school report card or progress report your child gets, and mark on your calendar when to expect those reports. Most schools have websites and e-mail addresses for teachers. Make sure you visit the website frequently and your e-mail address is up-to-date on the teacher's e-mail list. Both parents can be on the list to receive progress and grade reports.

This is another area where it is wise to gather information, especially if you think the other parent could be making things worse. Remember, just the facts. Keep track of problems that might happen when your child is at the other parent's house. Take note if after spending the night with the other parent, your child is tardy or doesn't turn in homework. Has your child lost books at the other parent's house? Has the custodial parent moved often and caused your child to be in many different schools?

Stress from parents' anger can cause emotional problems, too. Are you mad at the other parent and your child most of the time? Do you express your frustration about the other parent to your child?

Or is the other parent angry a lot? Does this cause your child to always be tense, uptight or afraid to make a mistake? Is this causing emotional problems for your child? Professional help is available. It works.

If there are problems of any kind, call or e-mail the teacher and schedule a teacher-parent conference. Include the other parent and remind them again just before the teacher conference. However, if the other parent stalls or won't attend, move forward on your own. While you want to be reasonable, your child's well-being is at stake. Don't wait too long. When you talk to the teacher, listen, take good notes and remain calm. Together, identify the problems and possible solutions. Does your child need testing? Remember every school is required to test children who may have learning issues. Ask the teacher where to go to get extra help for your child.

While one good conference with the teacher is a great step forward, don't stop there. Make sure you follow up and stay in touch with the teacher to work on these problems. Use e-mail to keep the other parent up to date and to make sure they are helping with the solution. For example, remind them to check the homework when the child is spending the night.

- **REFEREE'S RULE:** Having your child evaluated by a professional counselor or therapist is as normal as getting your child vaccinated.

- **PRACTICAL TIP:** If you suspect a gap or a problem, speak with an expert.

- **TALKING TIP:** "I think we should all go to counseling."

- **LEGAL TIP:** Public schools are required by law to provide services and an education to a child with any special needs.

Serious emotional or mental health problems

If you believe your child is experiencing problems in this area, this is no time for the self-help approach, church counselors or family friends. You need an expert. That is, a licensed, qualified professional to treat your child and help you and the other parent cope.

These problems will not fix themselves. Without professional help, your child will decline, his or her problems will get worse and your life will be a constant parade of unmanaged crises and disruptions. Insurance will usually pay for mental health care, so make sure you have the child on insurance before you start. Community mental health centers are also a good resource for help with emotional problems.

Small children with attention deficit disorder or hyperactivity literally cannot control their behavior without help. Without treatment, bipolar teenagers can have such mood swings that the highs can lead to bizarre behavior while the lows can lead to suicide. Sometimes, feelings of grief and abandonment are the root of the problem. When children (and adults) feel they can't succeed at anything, they spin out of control into feelings of failure, frustration and anger. Without help, this can cause disastrous behavior. Eating disorders often affect teenagers. Obsessive-compulsive behavior can cause a child to have both social and educational problems.

This is where you need a professional who can pinpoint the problem and offer treatment. Often, medication can help the child and manage the problems, but only a professional can determine this. Remember, it is *not* a badge of shame for the child to be on medication for attention deficit disorder or bipolar disorder. It is medicine for an illness, just as insulin is a treatment for diabetes or allergy medication is medicine for allergies. Take action!

At the same time, you may find *you* need some help and support, too. It's hard for parents when their children have emotional or mental health problems. You know something is just not right, but you don't know where to start to make things better. It's easy to stress out and continually ask yourself, "What am I doing wrong?" Sometimes the problems stem from all the change and instability that can result from a child's parents living apart. Even if you know being apart from the other parent is best for everyone, it's sometimes difficult to face up to problems this situation may cause your children. Being honest with yourself is the best policy. Taking action, both for your child and yourself, is critically important.

Where to start with mental health needs

- Get the school to do an evaluation if your child is school age. This is free.

- Get your insurance lined up and find out what is provided for mental health. Usually this is under your employee assistance program (EAP).

- Find a community mental health clinic if you do not have insurance coverage.

- Explain your concerns to the other parent by e-mail and copy the doctor, teacher or professional. List specific examples of the problem you see.

- Save the e-mail.

- Are there behavioral issues at school that are part of this? List them.

- Has the child moved a lot and had a very unstable life? Can you change that?

- Has there been a tragedy or drama in the child's life? Loss of a close relative or abandonment of a parent are examples.

- Is there a family history of mental illness?

- Do not try the self-help method of solving this. Get an expert.

10. Money. There is never enough.

Money is one roadblock you can expect. This always makes the top-ten list. Like visitation, this is such a huge issue there is an entire chapter (Chapter Ten) devoted to child support. Money, after all, is the number one thing couples argue about, and is often the main cause of conflict in any relationship. There is always something else children need, and there is always something more parents want them to have. When parents say an argument is not about money, it usually really *is* about money.

The biggest roadblock involving money usually comes when child support is not paid, paid late or it is not enough. It also comes when one parent is perceived as being a 'gold digger' who is using the child just to get money. It's a major roadblock when the dad thinks the mom got pregnant just to get child support (and that's hard to overcome). It's a major roadblock when the parent paying support thinks, or knows, the parent with the child is wasting the money (going to casinos, supporting a worthless boyfriend) or not spending the child support on their child. This can get ugly.

If at all possible, *stay in your lane* regarding money. That means get a court order setting child support based on state guidelines where you live. Stay in your lane by not complaining or criticizing how the other parent makes money or spends money. You cannot control what someone buys, nor can you oversee every dime spent.

Take the high road (or the highest you can afford) when it comes to money for your child. Pay the set child support on time. Always be generous when the child is with you and be generous at holidays and on birthdays. If you are the one who gets the child support, stay within your budget. If you don't have another source of income, get a job that will supplement the child support. Communicate with the other parent about the extras of raising a child, such as summer camp, school trips or braces. If at all possible, make these extras available for your child or split the cost fifty-fifty.

Be prepared to take action if the other parent doesn't pay the child support. If the court ordered child support is not paid, there is a process in every court for contempt. Make sure you follow the process carefully. Every child support enforcement agency in the country is required to attach bank accounts, garnish paychecks, attach IRS (Internal Revenue Service) checks and take away passports and licenses from a parent who does not pay court-ordered child support.

If that does not work, just wait and be patient. This obligation won't go away and the delinquent parent can't bankrupt child support. Everybody has to pay court-ordered child support eventually. When grandma dies and passes her house into an estate for the family to divide, a well-placed lien on grandma's house will prevent the house from being sold and inconvenience the entire family until the back child support is paid. Courts can place a lien on unemployment checks, social security checks and workers compensation checks to cover child support. This can all be handled by state attorneys who work for child support enforcement agencies.

Be forewarned, though: This process can be very slow, so figure out a way to survive while you wait. Whatever you do and however contentious money issues become, never complain or talk about child support to or in front of your child. Never punish the non-paying parent by withholding visitation with the child. That punishes your child, not the parent. (More about this in Chapter Ten)

> *Our son pays a respectable amount of child support every month to our granddaughter's mother. However, during the last week of almost every month, our granddaughter calls us and asks for food or money for school or something we can't possibly turn down. We know the mother quit her job because she thought she was going to get a role in a movie being shot in our city. The movie role was small and lasted about two months, then she started going out all the time with the artsy film people. We are happy to keep our granddaughter when the mom is doing this, but we resent being hit up for money every month.*

***

- **REFEREE'S RULE:** Money is not important as long as you have it.

- **PRACTICAL TIP:** Go to the child support department together to get it set up. Some agencies can do a consent order on the spot if you take proof of income, proper identification, proof of insurance and costs of childcare.

- **TALKING TIP:** "I think we should get child support paid through the system."

- **LEGAL TIP:** Child support enforcement agencies are in every state and every county. They represent any parent who files for child support or for collection of child support. You do not have to receive government assistance to get this service. However, if your child has received any type of government assistance then the non-custodial parent will be put on child support by your state. They will also help a parent put himself/herself on child support.

CHAPTER FOUR
What to Do About the Fight
The Options: Do You Fight or Do You Mediate?

A domestic fight is more than just a yelling and screaming argument. If it spins out of control and the parents absolutely cannot agree to work together to raise the children they have had together, the situation can spin into a legal battle of epic proportion with legal expenses so large you could have paid off your house or paid for your child's entire college education with what you paid the lawyers.

Before you hire a lawyer and tell him/her that you want to do whatever it takes to win, ask yourself this question: What is really in my child's best interest?

Deciding if it is worth going to court

When you are tempted to fight in court, there can be many issues that can distract you from the question of what's best for your child. How do you decide if you want to fight to the finish or just give up? Which approach do you take? When the other side is a bully, a control freak or totally wrong, doesn't someone need to stand up to him or her?

Consider, is this really in your child's best interest or is this your own personal issue?

How do you keep from looking weak? If looking weak is what matters, you will need to re-focus on what counts. Your child. How do you know what is really best for your child? Are we fighting for money? Pride? Ego? Reputation? All of the above?

Maybe it is a true battle involving your values. Perhaps the other parent uses drugs or is not ever able to get the child to school on time. Maybe the other parent is just plain crazy.

The only good reasons to fight in court for custody and/or visitation of your child are when the issues involve the following:

- Someone at the other parent's home is physically, emotionally or sexually abusive to your child.

- Someone at the other parent's home is abusing drugs or alcohol.

- The child has medical or educational issues, which the other parent will not address.

- The other parent has untreated severe mental health issues which are hurting your child.

- The parent with custody is in jail or going to jail.

- The parent with custody has a debilitating or terminal medical issue and is unable to parent your child.

- The other parent has abandoned your child.

Only under extreme situations such as these is it generally worth fighting to the finish.

More often, it is tempting to fight to the finish, particularly if you feel the other parent is a bully, control freak, totally wrong and/or way overdue for someone to stand up to him or her. Again, is that in your child's best interest or is that your personal issue?

You might be concerned about looking weak to the other parent. But again, is that in your child's best interest?

Chances are, if you are going to court to fight for custody and it's about money, pride, ego, reputation or concern about looking weak to the other parent, you are catering to your own personal issues—and not focusing on what is really best for your child.

These are bad reasons to fight in court for custody or visitation:

- You have a lot of money to spend on lawyers, discovery, depositions and trials.

- You think you can wear down the other side by days in court.

- You want to say lots of ugly, demeaning things in public where lots of people can hear it.

- You need to unload your emotional baggage in front of a judge and tell the other parent publicly how badly you have been treated, how hurt you are and what a scum-bag he or she is. (Have a wonderful pity-party.)

- This is really only about money. Unfortunately, there is never going to be enough.

Get help if you are the one with the Issues

At this point, I want to make an appeal to you if you are the parent with the problems and issues. Stop the fight and get help first. Getting help will strengthen your position. Getting help will make you a better person. Getting help will help your child. Professional help can make all the difference, so take action to do what's best for your child and best for you, too, in the long run.

- **REFEREE'S RULE:** Put your emotions aside and think carefully before you decide to go to court. I have seen dozens of families learn the hard, expensive way that the long-term bad feelings of a court battle are not worth it.

- **PRACTICAL TIP:** No matter how much you think you dislike someone and no matter how many bad thoughts you have, saying those thoughts in court, telling those bad things in front of a court reporter, formalizing it in a deposition, in other words spilling blood all over the floor never solves the problem.

- **TALKING TIP:** "I hate you, I hate you, I hate you, I hate you, I hate you, I hate you." Now, do you feel better? No, I didn't think so.

- **LEGAL TIP:** Discovery, interrogatories and depositions are legal means of getting information. A deposition is where the attorneys meet in a conference room without a judge and ask a witness questions under oath with a court reporter or on video. This is later used in court.

What else can you do? Mediate

What is mediation? Mediation, conducted by a neutral mediator who does not favor either side, helps parents find middle ground. It helps them reach mutually agreeable solutions without the emotional and financial expense of a full trial.

Mediation is where the mother and father (occasionally other parties are involved), with or without lawyers, meet with a neutral, trained person in a conference room that has breakout rooms. The mediator takes each parent alone, one at a time, into a conference room and hears their story without the other parent being present.

The mediator hears what the underlying emotional issues are. These are the "I've been done wrong" issues. Then, she or he helps the parents decide what they can agree upon. The mediator listens to what the parents do *not* agree upon. To work out the things they do not agree upon, the mediator then goes back and forth, meeting with each party in private, and works with each parent to find some middle ground.

What if the mediator recommends a guardian ad litem for your child?

A guardian ad litem is called a GAL. This is the attorney appointed by the court for the child. A mediator cannot appoint a GAL. Only a judge can appoint the GAL. A GAL is usually paid by both parties and only represents the child.

The mediator can ask the court to appoint this type of attorney for the child. The GAL will go out and talk with the child in private, visit teachers, interview both parents and independently investigate the problem issues. The mediator does not do those things. Some mediators will talk with an older child, but mediators never investigate. If there are medical problems to investigate, the GAL can see the medical records and report the problem areas. This must be done before the mediation, or the mediation gets postponed until the report of the GAL is complete. Usually, mediation takes one full day, however, when more information is needed or when a GAL is appointed to investigate, the process will take longer.

The advantages of mediation

The outcome of mediation is usually much better than the result of a week-long trial. With mediation, parents have more input and opportunity to design their schedules around their individual lives. The other advantages of mediation compared with going to court are:

- Parents help write the rules for raising their kids themselves. That is called a permanent parenting plan.

- Parents develop a clear understanding about their child-raising issues.

- Mediating is cheaper.

- Parents usually don't have a chance to say things in front of each other that will be permanently damaging. They may vent confidentially to the mediator.

- Parents avoid ruining what might remain of the good aspects of their relationship.

- Parents might still be able to talk in the end.

- Parents protect their children from sitting through the court system and being caught in the middle of their arguments.

- Parents can also agree that the mediator will be their parenting arbitrator in the future, to help mediate new disputes or change the plan to fit new circumstances. Because, remember: things *will* change.

Make sure you remember this important point: A mediation agreement can only be enforced by a court *if* it is taken before a judge and entered as a court order. Make sure the mediator is a lawyer who knows how to draft a final order of your agreement, or that he or she can get your order drafted by an attorney and ensure it is properly entered in court.

> *It was over. We both knew it. We've both made mistakes and done stupid things. We could spend days telling a judge about the crazy things each of us has done. We've both been irresponsible, but we've never put our child at risk. We are both good parents. We agree about almost everything except holidays. She expects every Christmas, every year, all season. No exceptions. I want all summer, from the day school is out to the day it begins in the fall. Period. Can we talk? What is the middle ground?*

***

There are several varieties of mediation style. Some mediators bring the parties together with the baby step approach. Others use the strategic method of mediation. Think about what might work best for you. Remember, you *do* want this to work. Fighting with the other parent is not supposed to be a full-time career. That is not an option.

> *Using baby steps, our mediator helps dad get two days at Thanksgiving, then mom gets two days in the fall, then dad gets part of Christmas right after school, and mom gets Christmas Day. Then mom gets Halloween and dad pays for plane tickets and the parties continue back and forth, giving, taking, step by step, etc.*

***

The strategic mediation style is where the mediator offers options, rather than suggestions, and sets one party up to really want one thing so badly this party is willing to give up something equally important in trade. For instance, one side trades New Year's for the Fourth of July, or birthdays for Thanksgiving.

> *Our mediator used strategic mediation to build up expectations. I wanted visitation all summer and she wanted visitation all Christmas. So our mediator forced me to ask myself, "How important is Christmas?" Well, the truth is I work in retail, so I am at the store until nine pm on Christmas Eve and I have to be back at eight am the day after Christmas. I'd rather just sleep all day on December twenty-fifth. It was really easy for me to give up Christmas. The trick was convincing her to give up the summer. So, I gave her the Fourth of July, including the week before and the week after. Then the mediator pointed out that summer with me would save a ton of summer day camp costs for her that the mediator convinced me to agree to pay. That finished the deal. They tell me that's how strategic mediation works.*

***

Mediation puts all of the cards on the table, it determines what is important to whom, then rearranges and shuffles the cards so everyone finally agrees to work together toward the goals agreed upon.

Why should I mediate? What's in it for me? If you are still asking yourself these questions, see below:

- **REFEREES RULE:** Three things make mediation worth your time: best outcome, least dramatic and cheapest. Plus, judges love for cases to be mediated and settled between the parties.

- **PRACTICAL TIP:** A day of mediation will usually accomplish more than a week in court.

- **TALKING TIP:** "Let's try mediation because we are most likely to get what is truly best for the kids."

- **LEGAL TIP:** Find a mediator who will charge a lower rate for the first three hours if you think your issues are limited and definable. For instance, some mediators will charge $150 per hour for the first three hours, then bump it up to $250 per hour after that. The goal is to make both parties seriously mediate. Show up ready to lay the issues on the table, plan to give and take, then give some more. It is so much cheaper to mediate than it is to fight.

I wanted to mediate but she wanted to fight, again. I offered to just pay for the mediation if she would show up. That was a disaster because instead of working together to resolve our problems, she spent the first three hours rehashing all of my sins and mistakes, then spent the next three hours bullying everyone and finally, we all left madder and more frustrated than when we arrived. I had to pay the bill. If we had split it fifty-fifty, both of us would have been trying to get out of there as soon as possible.

***

- **REFEREE'S RULE:** Mediation is always best if both sides have some skin in the game.

- **PRACTICAL TIP:** If both of you agree to *not* hire a lawyer and you both agree on a really good mediator, you can save a fortune and get to the same place.

- **TALKING TIP:** "We have some major issues to resolve. Let's agree we won't hire lawyers, and instead put our money on a mediator who will help us resolve our issues."

- **LEGAL TIP:** Make sure the mediator is a lawyer who knows how to draft a final order of your agreement or he or she can get your order drafted by an attorney and entered in court. *It is critical for you to follow up on that detail.* If there is no final order entered in court, a year or two from now when memories are mixed up, there will be no proof and no ability to enforce what you have agreed upon. Keep in mind in some states, the mediator cannot also be a lawyer for the parties.

Don't let your anger, your desire for revenge, or your thirst for a fight in court distract you from what's really important: your child. What you want for your child and for yourself should not be revenge, but a good life.

Thus, your goal for mediation should be to obtain a happy, safe, stress-free life, filled with opportunities for a good future for you and your child. Period. To get there, it is best to mediate and through mediation, have a clear plan with a clear understanding of holidays, schools, rules, trips and other issues that come up when you are living apart but raising a child together. Don't forget that final order, so your plan can stay alive and be enforced legally if necessary for the good of everyone involved.

CHAPTER FIVE

What to Do About a Lawyer
When and How to Get a Lawyer

Sometimes, there is no way around it. You must hire a lawyer.

In this chapter we skip the stories and offer you rules for the various steps of finding and hiring a good lawyer, what to expect and how to work effectively with that lawyer once he or she is hired. In general, it is important to be prepared, be brief and do not hide anything important from your lawyer. Remember, your lawyer is bound by law to keep what you say confidential.

When do you need a lawyer?

- When the other side gets a lawyer.

- When you know your relationship is over and it is going to get complicated.

- When your child is being mistreated, abused and/or neglected.

- When money starts to disappear.

- When all your friends tell you to get a lawyer.

- When you get arrested.

Where do you start?

1. Do *not* hire from billboards, advertisements or the back of the phone book.

2. Ask your friends.

3. Do not hire a lawyer who is supposed to be the meanest, toughest family lawyer in town. You need a negotiator, not a hired gun. You want someone who can make things happen for you without making everyone so mad they never speak to you again.

4. Call someone who knows a lawyer and ask that lawyer to give you three recommendations of lawyers you might interview.

5. Look for someone who does domestic/family law work only. This takes special skill. You don't want someone who also does real estate or criminal work.

6. Call the local bar association and ask for recommendations. Make sure the lawyer you are considering is a member in good standing of the bar association. Have there been any official complaints filed against your lawyer? Ask the bar association.

7. Look up your prospects on the internet.

8. A small firm with several lawyers is often your best bet. With a large law firm, you will be paying for the firm's high overhead costs. A one-person law firm means your prospective lawyer is not always available in a crisis.

9. Go to the family law court clerk or juvenile court clerk and ask for their recommendations.

How do you get a lawyer?

After you research him or her through friends, the internet and other resources and make sure he or she is a member in good standing of the bar association, it's time to pick up the phone and call for an appointment. Before you call, write down your facts and go over them in your mind, so you will stay on track and not ramble when you talk to the lawyer. A good lawyer will not want to take your case if you talk incessantly about unnecessary things. A bad lawyer will take your case, but charge you a lot more for all of the extra time your unnecessary talk takes.

1. Call the lawyer and ask for a brief appointment. Ask if there is a charge for the initial consultation or meeting. Some lawyers charge, some do not. Really good lawyers charge because they can and they are worth it.

2. A lawyer who is a calm problem solver will serve you better than a lawyer who fights to the finish. That being said, being assertive and in control are characteristics of a good lawyer.

3. Do not hire a lawyer who is always in fight mode. You do not want your lawyer to generate so much bad blood the fight just gets worse. Remember, *you* will still have to communicate with your ex long after the tough lawyer is gone.

4. Show up for the first appointment early. Have your file with all important documents already copied. Have a list of all of the parties, their ages and the issues. Appendix B at the end of this book will help you with all your facts. Make your list brief, using bullet points of the major issues.

5. Be ready to pay. Lawyers typically ask for a retainer, which is like a down payment, depending on how complicated your case might be. A retainer is money paid up front, which is then used up as the case goes along. It is applied to the balance. Lawyers serve a purpose and provide good advice. It is not free.

How do you work with your lawyer efficiently?

1. Remember, lawyers charge by the hour, so it is to your advantage to use the time efficiently.

2. Your lawyer is not your psychologist.

3. Your lawyer is not your loan agent.

4. Your lawyer is not going to change your ex and suddenly make him or her a reasonable, thoughtful, perfect person.

5. Your lawyer can only take the train-wreck you are in and pull it apart one car at a time.

6. Do not call your lawyer when you are angry about your situation. A pity party with your lawyer will be expensive and will not help solve your legal problems.

7. The more organized you are and the more clearly you explain your problems, the better job your lawyer can do for you.

8. Always tell your lawyer the mistakes you have made. Tell it all, briefly, and only one time. This could be the most important information you give your lawyer. What you tell your lawyer is protected by attorney-client confidentiality laws.

9. List the offenses of your ex clearly, briefly and once.

10. A lawyer cannot guarantee how a judge will rule. Remember, the lawyer will not offend a judge on your behalf, because he or she must go back in front of that same judge again on other cases.

11. Set deadlines for every event and a follow up to make sure this does not drag on forever.

What should you expect from your lawyer?

1. Your lawyer should accompany you to court hearings and procedures.

2. Your lawyer should know the facts of your case and be able to advise you on the probable or merely possible outcome of your case. This allows you to make good choices about the direction you should take and the options you should choose.

3. Your lawyer should help you work toward a solution, a schedule and an outcome which will help your children. That is the main point.

4. You should expect a monthly bill for charges from the lawyer. The bill will be paid out of the retainer fee until the retainer runs out. A retainer fee is like a pre-paid credit card. It is a lump sum you pay to hire the lawyer.

What should you <u>not</u> expect from your lawyer?

1. A miracle.

2. Free advice.

3. A cleanup for your mess.

4. Cover for lies or untruths.

5. A willingness to work for *you* to the detriment of your child.

6. Twenty-four, seven availability.

7. Psychological counseling.

8. Cover for any criminal or potential criminal behavior.

- **LEGAL TIP:** Don't be late for court. *Ever.*

CHAPTER SIX

What to Do About Your Thoughts
Controlling the Mind Talk

You wouldn't be reading this book if your life were perfect. And if you and everyone else were perfect, we wouldn't have courts, lawyers or mediators. Even churches would be out of business. We have all seen those church signs that say, "Only sinners need apply." Applying at the church door is an approach that might work for some, but the point is for you to recognize we all have imperfections and we are all trying to be better.

Unfortunately, feeling bad about being imperfect can quickly get out of hand.

Self-destructive mind talk begins when people can't stop beating up on themselves for the things they have done or not done. Does this sound familiar? Here are some typical guilt trips single parents lay on themselves:

- I'm a lousy parent.

- I don't see my kid enough because I work so much.

- My child is in daycare too much.

- My babysitter is not great, my kids hate her.

- I'm so impatient around my child.

- I'm too tired to be creative and fun.

- I can't afford the basics, much less all of the stuff other kids have.

- I'm always late paying child support, and I resent paying it.

- My child is such a burden and I hate myself for feeling that way.

- My parents help too much and I cannot seem to take the lead.

- His or her new spouse is better at parenting than I am.

Well, by definition a single parent is missing someone, for better or worse. Sometimes the alternative is worse. Thus, putting the past behind you is one of the first steps. Once the dust settles and everyone has his or her place, the absence of a person who always makes you feel bad will be like the absence of thunder and lightning during a warm spring shower. Stop beating yourself up. Move on. But do you still find yourself having times when your mind just won't stop replaying bad scenes or rehashing other possibilities? You can't quit thinking about negative things and your mind talk becomes destructive. Do these stories sound like you?

Things would have been different if I had only not lied about it. Had I admitted my mistake and apologized, I might have gotten a break. But I handled it all so badly. I'm such an idiot. I'm stupid.

***

I shouldn't have done what I did. I feel so bad about everything. I wish I could take back everything I said and did. I keep messing up and I keep going over and over everything in my mind.

***

I'm such a lousy parent and person. I haven't done any of the things other parents have done with their children. My child hasn't had half what other kids get and I'm so lousy when I finally do something. I never read stories to my child. We don't

84

go to the playground or do artsy stuff. I just sit around and complain.

***

This person's habit of complaining instead of doing something probably started long before he or she had a child. Have you found yourself thinking like this? When did you start beating yourself up? Is that your life's pattern? Do you whine and complain a lot? Does *everybody* have it better than you? Do you think everything about your life sucks? Do you think your child always messes up? Ouch.

Constant whining and complaining becomes a bad habit, a pattern, a personality trait. It is a character flaw. You find you always see the glass as half empty. Nothing is ever satisfactory. Everyone else always gets the breaks. You are always the underdog who is being snubbed. Are you a bad luck magnet? Do you always get caught misbehaving when everyone else gets away with murder? Do you think your siblings got treated better than you did? Do you bristle at friends' casual comments and take offense easily?

Low self-esteem does that to a person. It keeps you always on edge and always feeling put down. Low self-esteem can stick you with mind talk that can get you down and keep you down.

It is particularly easy for this to happen to single parents in a world where a mom-and-dad-under-one-roof family is considered the norm. Sometimes single parents are heartbroken over the separation between themselves and the other parent. For others, separating from the other parent was the best thing that ever happened to them.

How do you stop?

Whatever the circumstances, getting the past behind you is one of the first steps to improving your self-esteem. Once the other parent has moved out, it is time for you to *move on*. Often, this takes some professional counseling. Getting private, individual help will also help you learn to manage destructive mind talk. Having a counselor to talk with will especially help you cope with your past when you have been abused or mistreated.

- **PRACTICAL TIP:** Explore what your insurance will cover for professional counseling or find out what free counseling is available in your city. Some churches offer professional counseling and you pay based on your income. Always get a counselor who is licensed and not just a minister.

What can you do about self-destructive mind talk when this is how you see the world? Where do you start? Here are some practical ways:

- Tell yourself you will not surrender to low self-esteem. And don't.

- Do not allow yourself the luxury of complaining. No one wants to hear it.

- Go to a counselor who specializes in self-esteem and depression problems. The two go hand-in-hand. People who have low self-esteem often get depressed. Don't try to do this by yourself.

- Do not let yourself ever believe you deserve bad treatment.

The blame game

Blame is such an easy past time. It is the way most people with self-esteem issues cope with feeling bad. They blame themselves and feel guilty, then, to get some relief, they blame somebody else. Blaming others gives a person a way out.

You see this happen with children who have self-esteem issues. They begin acting out. They become the class clown or take on a teacher whom they are sure is picking on them. Eventually, their perception that people in authority don't like them becomes reality. When they are always showing off, others begin to feel they are the problem. People in authority such as teachers, police or bosses at work then see them as difficult and the source of all problems. It becomes a self-fulfilling prophecy. This story has every example. The next stories show really big mistakes.

I've never been an early riser. I always slept through early classes in college and lost a couple of jobs because I could not get there on time. Morning is just not my time. So when I got custody of my little boy and he had to be at pre-school by eight am, that was almost impossible. We were late every day. The teachers had a meeting with me. I couldn't change. My mother was always late to stuff, too. I'm just doing what she did. No one would offer to call and wake me. Friends should have helped. My apartment building is so loud we were always up late and were tired in the morning. Not learning to get up in the morning and get to things on time has cost me a lot. I'm such a loser. I flunked out of college. I can't get a good recommendation from any job I have had because they always say I can't get to work on time. Now, not getting my child to school on time might cost me custody of him. It's really not my fault!

***

- **REFEREE'S RULE:** Don't blame others for your own mistakes.

- **PRACTICAL TIP:** Never blame your mother. It sounds so lame.

- **TALKING TIP:** "I am so sorry I did not get here on time. I won't let it happen again."

- **LEGAL TIP:** This one is so important we say it twice: Don't be late to court. *Ever.*

I lived in an apartment building that was like a college fraternity house. Everyone was young and partying a lot. When I got my little boy, I should have moved to a nice neighborhood and quit living like a wild partier. I wanted to stay where I knew people, so my kid just went with me to everything I did. We were always up late, rarely doing kid stuff and mostly doing what young twenty-something people do. Heck, my child can't count or tell kids' stories, but he knows baseball and beer. He's really smart and has picked up everything I know, which is scary.

***

- **REFEREE'S RULE:** Exposing your child to adult situations is bad parenting. Children should be home in bed and not being dragged around behind a drinking or drunk parent.

- **PRACTICAL TIP:** Move.

- **TALKING TIP:** "I just need some guidance and I am going to parenting classes, which has helped a lot. Also, I have moved and gotten away from all the old stuff I used to be around."

- **LEGAL TIP:** If a young child drinks beer, smokes, swallows a drug, then the parent can be charged with neglect, abuse or contributing to the delinquency of a minor. You can go to jail for exposing a young child to these things.

When behavior gets really destructive

When we got to court the first time, I was so angry I just lost it. I started yelling and cussing in the hall and I think the judge heard it. Then I slammed the courtroom door and broke the glass and as we walked through the parking lot, I saw a car that looked like the grandparent's car. It wasn't, but I keyed it anyway.

***

- **REFEREE'S RULE:** Getting counseling for anger management or emotional problems always shows a desire to improve and change bad behavior. Get professional help before it is court ordered.

- **TALKING TIP:** "The stress of these matters has gotten to me and I recognize I need help. I have begun having sessions with Doctor Therapist. It has already made a huge difference."

- **LEGAL TIP:** If your bad behavior has resulted in separate legal issues, such as driving under the influence, assault charges or vandalism charges, talk with your lawyer about the best way to get those charges dismissed. Counseling is always good, but don't let it appear to be an admission to a criminal charge.

Finding a way out of destructive thinking

Feeling bad, beating yourself up and carrying regrets is no way to live. It just plain makes you a loser. It keeps you depressed. It takes away your confidence. It makes you feel crummy.

This mind talk, while still negative, is headed in the right direction at the end:

> *My family thinks I've screwed up everything I've touched. They are right. I do make a lot of mistakes. I need to get a break. I hate myself for these screw-ups. My family is right. I do bring most of it on myself. Now, where do I start over?*

***

Where *do* you start over?

Putting together a plan is not about rehashing everything you did wrong. It is about taking out a clean sheet of paper, writing number one up in the corner and starting from the beginning with a new plan. Get help thinking up fresh ideas. Remember the milestones? Where do you see yourself in five years? Still in a dead-end job or doing what you love? If that is teaching and coaching at a local school, what steps can make that happen? You decide.

In order for a plan to be realistic, a person has to look at the past and consider the options. Despite that, never dwell on the past and don't use past failure as an excuse to procrastinate.

> *I want to be a doctor but must consider the fact that I never passed biology because I was too busy partying the night*

before the final exam. Do I just beat myself up over my past biology performance?

***

No. This person needs to move on to another option.

- **REFEREE'S RULE:** Always have a plan B. This is the plan that might turn out to be the best thing for you anyway. Think about what you want to do, not what your family wants you to do or what your father did. List the steps for arriving at your goal. Then, come up with another goal. Pursue both of them. It usually takes education. Where do you go from here to achieve what you want and what is realistic?

- **TALKING TIP:** "I now have a plan I can follow. Would you help me stay focused on this plan so I can make it work?"

- **LEGAL TIP:** Get professional help to deal with sleep problems or problems that keep holding you back. Depression or anxiety disorder will keep you down. Get help.

Now, look at the guilt list at the beginning of this chapter. If some of these complaints and problems are yours, own it and work on fixing it. Is your child's babysitter not the best? What is the problem? How can you improve on your childcare? Could you get a family member to help, or is that the problem? Now might be the time to find someone new and more dependable.

- **PRACTICAL TIP:** If childcare issues are holding you back, find another parent or two and form a babysitting co-op. You help each other and share taking care of each other's kids. The babysitting co-op might also be a good source of support and advice. You can ask them how they avoid being impatient and cranky with their kids. The co-op might also be a good place for getting a break. However, be aware you must do your share, too. Can you handle a group of kids easier than just your own?

What about being tired and impatient? It is easy to be cranky. Look at your schedule and try to fit in a little more rest time and a little exercise time. Then, look at yourself and figure out what triggers your impatience. Is it stress at work or stress at home or both?

How to handle the ones who seem to have it all

When the grandparents or the new spouse seem to always do it better than you, don't let that distract you from what really counts to your child. You need to realize your child really just wants your time, not your stuff or your entertainment. Bike rides, picnics and outings that are creative might give you a chance to have quality time. Yes, the grandparents might have access to a swimming pool and thus, they are able to throw the best birthday party ever. Don't go and sit off to the side and sulk. Show your child how to be grateful and appreciative.

Find creative ways to do this. For example, let's say the new spouse of your ex is having a birthday. You and your child make a cake/cupcakes/cookies or a gift together. You enjoy the activity of making and decorating. You teach the value of showing appreciation to someone who is helping care for your child. You show your child how you are not jealous or petty, but thoughtful and grateful. When you teach your child to be thoughtful to others, it will come back to you.

- **PRACTICAL TIP:** "Slice and bake" is just fine when you and your child want to make cookies together. Don't try to be perfect. You and your child can have a wonderful dining experience by ordering pizza. Plus, you can often find coupons for cake mixes and canned icing. Enjoy and eat while you cook. Most of all make it easy and have fun.

- **PRACTICAL TIP:** You and your child can prepare a photo collage or a hand-made thank you for the grandparents. Make this a thank you card that shows you and your child appreciate the extra, un-expected, not required help they provide. Treat them as people to thank, not as a parent who is *expected* to do such helpful things. Thus, you take control and are the leader. You are appreciative and teach your child to be grateful for extra help. Teach your child how to treat others. That is how he or she will later treat you.

While you are doing the above thoughtful, considerate things with your child, don't let any negative talk ruin the moment. Resist the temptation to say something tacky about the extra attention, extra money or extra stuff the other person has. Remember this is a teachable moment that requires you to be positive. Your glass is half full while you enjoy the richness of a fun activity with your child.

Remember, the grandparents may have a swimming pool and the ex's new spouse may have a talent you don't possess. But, never forget you are your child's parent and to your child, nothing is more important or more meaningful than spending time with you.

CHAPTER SEVEN
What to Do About Your Attitude
Fake It!

When we say fake it, what are we talking about? Living a lie? Being a fraud? *No.*

What are we faking? If you are raising a child with someone and you live apart, there are many times when putting on your nicest or strongest face, regardless of whether you really feel that way, is best for everyone, especially your child. Your child is the one you need to protect from negative stuff. That's what we are talking about.

Get ready to force yourself to be nice, pleasant and agreeable, regardless how you really feel, in the following areas: (Practice if you have to.)

- **Fake it** to your ex.
- **Fake it** to his or her new love.
- **Fake it** to your ex-in-laws.
- **Fake it** being in control with your teenager.
- **Fake it** being in charge as a parent.

We've all heard the expression, "Honesty is the best policy." But sometimes too much honesty is *not* the best policy. Your daughter is all dressed up for a party and you tell her she looks beautiful, when in truth her outfit makes her look silly. It is like lying when your best friend asks, "Do these pants make me look fat?"

You are looking at someone you really don't like, but you force your face to look totally neutral and friendly. It's like always telling your grandmother that you love her fruitcake.

Faking it means forcing your voice not to have an ounce of dripping sarcasm when you talk with your ex or his or her newest love interest. It means, even if you feel way too weak to enforce your parenting rules, you can still say with absolute, unwavering certainty, "No, you cannot have a boy/girl slumber party at my house. Nor can you attend one at someone else's house. That is final."

TALKING TIP: "Because I said so." End of discussion. Whew.

Revealing your true feelings in these situations would not help and, in fact, would serve to hurt people's feelings, antagonize someone you are going to have to work with or undermine your own authority. Sometimes, it is best all-around to keep your true feelings under wraps. Honesty is *not* always the best policy.

When you pretend to be pleasant to your ex and when you are nice no matter how you really feel, you become a better person. Most importantly, your child benefits from watching you behave with real class. Your child benefits from your calm, positive attitude. Your child will not have anxiety or stress that comes with dreading every time his or her parents meet because they act so badly. Your child should never, ever suspect you dislike the other parent so much.

Christmas is still a traumatic time for me. I have flashbacks of how terrible my parents acted to each other. I dreaded it then. My stomach would hurt as we prepared for my other parent to show up, always late, on purpose. Why did they insist on having it together? I still get that same stomachache at the thought of the holidays we were forced to share.

***

The first step is to keep your mouth shut if you are tempted to blurt out negative feelings. Make a promise to yourself that you will not go there. Ever. If you must vent, choose a trusted relative or friend who will keep his or her mouth shut. Next, paste on that smile. Keep it turned up. Everyone looks better with a smile. That is living well.

Others will think more highly of you if you do not bad mouth the other side. People will only pity you if you refer to the other woman as a tramp and a whore. Guess what? She's not the one who looks bad. *You* look bitter, mean and spiteful. Friends will feel sorry for you, or worse, they will think, "She's so mean, I can see why he left her."

A better approach is to never mention the other side. Smile. Fake it. Say nothing. Plan something else. Change the dynamics so that it doesn't have to be this way.

> *He was clearly unfaithful. People knew he was sleeping around. His wife had always been a strong, smart woman and she was devastated to be so humiliated and powerless. She resented friends and acquaintances who knew about the other women and seemed to protect him. She could see it in their eyes they pitied her. At first, she could not help bashing him to her friends. When she saw they pitied her more, she got so mad she decided to try a new plan. She stopped bashing him, and made it her business to say nothing about him and his ways. People would pry, trying to get her to gossip, but she resisted. She began living her own life, setting her own goals and going after those goals. He didn't exist except in polite conversation, and polite conversation doesn't trash talk. People stopped feeling sorry for her and instead felt sorry for him as a loser who messed up a good thing.*

***

The moral of that story is all about polite conversation. Polite conversation does not talk trash. It stays on the high road. Fake it. Smile… even if it kills you.

What if you are so mad you could scream? Find *one* trusted person who can keep his or her mouth shut. In bad situations it is important to have someone who hears you and gives you good, objective advice. You need to be able to complain, but *only* to that one special person. Obviously, *never* vent to your new boyfriend or girlfriend. He or she doesn't want to hear about your ex all the time.

- **REFEREE'S RULE:** Don't discuss your ex with others. They will pity you.

- **PRACTICAL TIP:** Get one very close, personal friend or family member such as a sister or brother you can talk with and vent to. That person can help you with your options and your plans for the future.

- **TALKING TIP:** "Sis, I need to scream. Let me tell you the latest. If I can just get this out of my system, I can go to work, smile and not talk about it."

- **LEGAL TIP:** Protect your money and your credit. If you think your relationship is ending, put your money where it will not vanish. Require two signatures on a savings account, one being *yours*. Change passwords. Direct deposit your paycheck into your account only. Protect your car. Call credit-card companies and close your accounts to all new charges. Try to get six months of rent saved up. Open one emergency credit card that only you know about.

Breaking up is not always in your best interest, especially in a bad economy in which you can't afford to break up. Staying together can be worse, but you may not have any choice. Whether you break up or stay together for practical reasons, professional help to deal with emotional issues will give you focus and strength. Expect to be angry, mad, depressed, sad and/or easily frustrated with others. These feelings won't last forever if you get help. Remember to focus on where you will be in five years. Remember those milestones we discussed in the beginning. They are still part of your life.

A clear exception to this is when there is abuse. An abusive relationship is bad for you, but it is especially bad for your kids. When children live in a home where their parent is being mistreated, they are victims just like the parent. They cannot be exposed to that without developing major problems. It is traumatic for everyone who witnesses and experiences abuse. Leave. Get help. Take action. *Fake being strong for your child's own good.*

Getting a grip on your outbursts benefits your child as well. Fake being happy around your kids. When all else fails, force yourself to hide your anger and frustration in front of your child. Try not to let it leak out even when they fail to feed the dog or don't make their beds. Keep your anger at the other parent from becoming anger at your child for other things.

Remember, if you are anxious, angry and bitter, your children will carry those emotions, too. They will have no idea why they feel this way and will often act out and misbehave just to get it out of their system.

Faking it is also part of good parenting. Every single day, you must tell your child he or she is the smartest child you know. You must tell your little girl she is the prettiest girl you know and she can achieve whatever she wants in life. You must tell your little boy he is the best ever. Always remind him he is smart, strong, clever and handsome. No matter how weak or frail they may seem, you must always tell your children they are wonderful and you are so happy to have them. Their play was better than anything on Broadway. Their singing was the music of angels. If you tell them that every day, it will become the truth. Let them hear you brag about them to family and friends, too. Start today if you are not already doing this. It is never too late to make a difference.

Complimenting your child and bragging on your child constitutes good parenting. If you need to fake it in some areas, know you are doing it for the best reason: building up your child's confidence and self-esteem.

Faking it sometimes involves taking your children to church, temple or synagogue, whether you yourself believe in God or not. Shop around until you find a place that is uplifting and spiritual, a place where you can find something you like, whether it's the music or the coffee hour. Most important, find a spiritual place your children like. Make sure it has a youth director and good programs for kids. Make sure your child fits in with the other kids. Does he or she feel at home there? Larger churches often have a counselor who can speak with children if they get depressed or anxious. Look for that person and get to know the counselor from the beginning. It will be easier to get an appointment if you need one later when the counselor already knows you.

Giving your child a spiritual base gives him or her a tool to help cope with the emotional issues involved with your separation. It helps on a lot of fronts. It might help you, too, whether you believe or not. This story shows the advantage of faking it.

His mom had a life we knew nothing about. We thought she was waitressing on Friday nights to make extra money, but actually she was prostituting. She got a two-year prison sentence. He is devastated. She was a really good mother to him, always listening to him. He really misses her. On her birthday, he cried himself to sleep. I thought it might help to get him in a youth group at a church, but they shunned him because of her. We were done with church people. Then, I ran across a group at a smaller church and they are really good to him. They helped him realize love conquers all. They have assigned him a special confidential mentor to help him deal with his loneliness, frustration, anger and confusion. It is good for him. I don't believe, but I go to church with him. I can fake it for now. Maybe I'll believe later.

***

- **REFEREE'S RULE:** Positive spiritual experiences give children strength and ability to cope. It gives you something to do.

- **PRACTICAL TIP:** Make sure the youth group covers your child's interests. If their big focus is sports and your child hates sports, find another group.

- **TALKING TIP:** "We only talk about his mother with his counselor." That shuts everyone up and lets them know he is being taken care of.

- **LEGAL TIP:** Taking a child to church always looks good in court.

Confident parenting is harder solo

In a two-parent household, when Mom says, "Do what your father told you to do," she can say that with much determination and conviction. It is so easy to be a confident parent when there are two of you. But in a single-parent household, when you are out-numbered, it is so easy for a child——and especially a teenager——to wear you down. They start with negotiating, then shift the argument to alternative plans, then bring up what you did back in the day. It can be very challenging to stay on course.

Another challenge is you never know at the time whether you are getting it right in the relentless job of parenting. You will not know until years later if you hit the target or the target hit you as a parent. The situation is even more difficult when parents are not on the same page. When the other parent is always harsher than you, more lenient than you, or simply absent on the major issues a parent has to decide, it is so difficult to be confident. Once again, just fake it. You can do it.

Remember, one factor over which you always have control is your own behavior. Kids are always watching and won't hesitate to throw your own mistakes in your face when they are trying to get their own way. This is why you should always keep your own behavior good in front of your children. Don't get drunk in front of your child or otherwise give them ammunition to use against you in the future. They will say "You got drunk just last week so what's the big deal about me getting beer from the older kids in the neighborhood?" Stop smoking. Get off the pills. Get help if you need it. Counseling is confidential. And, the 12-Step programs are free.

You must be strong when negotiating with your child, because the limitations you impose are for his or her own good. If you don't feel strong or confident when laying down the law, you must fake it convincingly. The potential consequences of being wishy-washy are too great. This story shows that a parent should follow instincts.

Camping in the back yard is such an old-fashioned, fun idea. Kids have done it for years. So when my eleven-year-old son asked to have a camp-out slumber party in the back yard, I said yes. Then, when he told me who was coming, I realized something was up. I had that funny feeling this was not a good idea, so I said no. He argued and argued until I said okay, as long as they stuck to certain rules. Then he talked me out of inviting an older boy to supervise them overnight. Everything seemed fine and I checked on the boys at midnight, then again at two. All was quiet. Then, about four, the police knocked on my door, wanting to know who was at my house. I led them to the back yard where everyone appeared to be sound asleep. We soon found they were only pretending to be asleep and had been out vandalizing our neighborhood. Five houses on our street had been egged. The fences of several neighbors had black spray paint on them. Someone had taken a brick and shattered the large picture window at the home of the most frail, elderly woman on our street, along with her sense of security and well-being. It was pure, mean vandalism. The boys started denying they were involved and blaming each other. I called my son's other parent and the other boys' parents and they all got mad at me for not lying to the police to protect their children. It was a mess. If only I had been strong, trusted my instincts and said no to the camp-out from the beginning.

***

What a mess. This behavior is going to mean delinquency charges that could show up as a criminal record whenever these boys apply to college or try to get a job. Luckily, this won't appear on their permanent records as adults and a lawyer may be able to get the charges removed from their juvenile record. This parent has to be strong now and make sure this boy feels the consequences of what he has done. He may be too young to get a job and pay for the damage, however, he is not too young to mow the lawn of every person vandalized for the entire next summer. He should have to go to counseling with the elderly woman whose window he and his friends broke. She will need it. He will, too.

- **PRACTICAL TIP:** Before you do anything in a crisis, call your most trusted person, that aunt, uncle, brother, sister, friend or lawyer. An objective third party will help.

- **TALKING TIP:** "I don't want to talk with anyone until I have gotten advice from my most trusted advisor, aunt, uncle, brother, sister, friend or lawyer."

- **LEGAL TIP:** A situation like this will lead to delinquency charges that will not be on his permanent record as an adult. However, every college application and job application will ask about arrests in the past. It will be on a juvenile record, although it may be possible and will take an attorney, to get it expunged or erased. It might be worth the expense of an attorney to see if this is possible.

CHAPTER EIGHT

What to Do About Changes
Change is Guaranteed, So Be Prepared

It doesn't take a crystal ball to look five years or 10 years down the road and predict some things that are almost guaranteed to happen. Whether you have a crystal ball or not, it's still a good idea to think ahead carefully. When you are aware of what is likely to happen and see it coming, you can prepare for it. Then, five years from now, you can say, "Yup, saw that comin'." No surprises.

Here is the referee's list of changes that are guaranteed in the years ahead, or at least very, very likely:

- One or both parents get married.

- Other children are born or come with the marriage.

- Children become teenagers or adults.

- Somebody loses their job.

- A grandparent or close relative dies.

- Someone moves.

It is worth your time to think ahead about how you will cope with big changes like these, so you are not caught by surprise.

Time to get back into the workbook mode. These topics, along with answer space are at Appendix E, "The Changes" for you to print, or at www.singleparentreferee.com. When these things happen to you, you will have a place to take notes and keep information.

One or both parents get married

If the other parent gets married, don't jump to negative conclusions that the situation will be bad. Work to make this a good relationship. Unless the situation is extremely unhealthy, making friends with the new spouse is a lot smarter than looking for a reason to feel slighted or wounded. Why? This person can help with driving, picking up and dropping off. This person could take your side on teenage problems. This person is going to have contact with your child and influence over how your child is raised.

Of course, nobody says making friends with your ex's new spouse is easy, but you can do it. (For tips, go back to Chapter Seven, "Fake It.")

He married a woman who was just weird. We have nothing in common. There's nothing wrong with her, but she has her hair dyed jet black and wears nothing but purple all of the time. When our daughter came home from a weekend visit, she got out of the car and I almost fainted. That woman had dyed my ten-year-old daughter's hair jet black and now my daughter was wearing purple. I was livid. Thing is, she is very sweet to my daughter, who now looks forward to going to her dad's. She helps me with childcare anytime I need it.

***

- **PRACTICAL TIP:** Hair grows out.

- **TALKING TIP:** "I really appreciate everything you do for Sissy. She enjoys visiting her dad, thanks to you. In the future, however, please don't change her hair until you talk with me about it first."

Sometimes, the situation is extremely difficult and it is just not possible to make friends with that spouse, or to even try. If the other person was the home-wrecker, the one who took your loved one away, it may not be possible for this relationship to be positive. In that case, it's best to attempt to have little or no contact with the new spouse. Don't set yourself up to be miserable.

Be prepared, though, because you *will* have to have contact with this person at times, especially if there is joint custody or visitation in the picture. Put on your seatbelt, because it can be a bumpy ride. It may be a good time to re-read Chapter Seven, "Fake It," and line up the person who will be your go-between, as discussed in Chapter Three under communications.

If you are the one getting married, you have different challenges as you introduce a new player in the game of parents living apart but raising a child together. If they haven't already met, as a matter of courtesy, introduce your new partner to the other parent. The best thing is to set up a meeting at a pleasant, neutral place. This will set the trend for how you deal with a lot of future discussions. My recommendation is a table at a comfortable, predictable, inexpensive restaurant. Everyone can have a muffin and cup of coffee. You do not have to sit through an entire meal. It is pleasant. You are not standing in a parking lot. No one's house is invaded. The child will not walk in on you. Talk pleasantly. Write down what you want to discuss so you don't leave out something important.

Think about what you would want to know if the shoe was on the other foot (and it will be someday). Explain where your new spouse works, where you will now live if this involves a move, what children he or she has, their ages and issues, their schools and visitation schedule. Discuss how your new spouse or partner can help for the benefit of all. Explain when and why you two will not be available to help, if there is such a time. If there is going to be a change in how you both communicate, discuss it. Don't make your child the messenger. Use e-mail and text messaging a lot.

Other children are born or come with the marriage

Movies with a "yours, mine, and ours" family theme may be cute and clever, but the reality of a mixed family is seldom so adorable. In actuality, it is a hugely stressful and awkward situation for children to have stepsiblings forced to share what used to be their personal space. How would you feel if a stranger moved into your room? That is exactly how a child feels, only more helpless in dealing with it. These stories show the stress of blended families.

I married a great guy who has two kids by his first wife. Then we had a baby, plus my child from my ex. We have a house full. There is no possibility for private rooms, much less private school now unless my ex wants to pay for it all. We have been told my child is a gifted tennis player and could go to college on a tennis scholarship if we work on that. Where do we start?

***

After we split up, she got pregnant again. The second dad was a good guy, but because he travels for work, he is rarely home. She had some problems with the pregnancy, so our child spent a lot of time with me. Then, after the baby was born, she was depressed, so our child stayed with me longer than either of us planned. The depression, health problems and loneliness made her house a really sad place to be. When our child spent time with her, he would come back so sad, worried and anxious about how she and the baby were living. I recommended she get some counseling. She lashed out at me like I was evil. I think all the medication has changed her personality. Sometimes I worry she might do something crazy.

***

The reason to have the restaurant conference is so the grown-ups can talk about all the issues in a reasonable manner. Discussing private school tuition well before it is due is best. Doing this in a manner that logically explains what all the factors are might not make everyone happy, but it is a lot better than waiting until the check is due to the school and then sending a text message that it won't be paid. That is *not* the way to handle it.

Planning for the tennis career will also take a face-to-face conversation. Who will be the best parent to manage this child's talent? Maybe it would be best to ask Uncle Harry, who played tennis in college, to be his mentor. Maybe he'll take this on as a special project. However, if you don't have an Uncle Harry, then discuss how you can get this gifted child to lessons and such—while you also deal with a new baby. Don't forget to ask other parents and grandparents. True, this is a lot to deal with, but this is a wonderful life.

Children become teenagers or adults

It's as if aliens have invaded their bodies when children become teenagers. They begin pushing, or should I say shoving, away from you. They reject things they always wanted in the past. They will want to test your rules and try out other alternatives. They may reject you and want to hang out more at the home of the other parent. If the other parent is a virtual stranger, the teenager may want to explore getting to know him or her.

One thing most teens have in common is they don't want supervision, yet they really need supervision at this age. They will pick the most lenient parent and try to stay there the most. They will choose the parent who is the least alert and make that parent their cover for all activities. They will long for the parent who has been the least attentive. They will seek out a parent who might have been absent for many years. Buckle up. It happens to the best of them and it can happen to you. This story could go in many directions.

> *My son Jason had never really known his dad, who got a job out of the country when I got pregnant. When he returned to the United States, he came to visit twice. Our son started getting on the computer with his dad and they talked a lot. He wanted to suddenly be a dad. I said, "Sure." We invited him for Jason's sixteenth birthday. My son was thrilled. All he could talk about was his dad.*

***

Somebody will have a job crisis

In a bad economy, no one's job is safe. Employment can change with no notice whatsoever. One day you've got a great, well-paying job and the next day the company is out of business. Whether the economy is good or bad, jobs are not perfect and sometimes people can only take so much, no matter how much they need the money. Quitting happens. Sometimes it's a matter of having one's hours cut or changed so working hours no longer fit in with family life. If one of you lost your job next week, could you survive? This story doesn't make it easier.

We felt terrible when Jason's dad did not show or call for Jason's 16th birthday. He finally called, but I was so mad, I ignored his phone call and deleted his message. Then a letter arrived, telling us the day before he was to leave to visit Jason, his business filed for bankruptcy and he was ordered by the bankruptcy court to be present for a legal proceeding. He sent newspaper clippings to prove it. Now, he reports he is unemployed and too embarrassed to visit because he has no money. The newspaper clipping shows him and others being escorted from the business. It obviously was a big deal and we believe him. The sad thing is he had nothing stored up for a crisis.

***

Learn a lesson from the experience of Jason's dad. Increase the odds that you can weather a period of unemployment by getting yourself stable. As tempting as it is, do not spend more money than you have. Don't buy the biggest house unless you really have the money to pay for it. Financial experts recommend saving up an emergency fund large enough to cover you for six months. That is often hard for families to manage, but if you do this while times are good, you will be glad you did when times turn bad.

A grandparent or close relative will die

When a close relative dies it can be a big blow to you, your child and to your support system. It is especially tough if you love that person and have depended on him or her to help you raise your child. You will also experience grief over the loss in unexpected and upsetting ways. This is an important time to talk to your child and listen, especially if this is a person, such as a grandparent, that your child loved and will miss, too. The child may be grieving and if you didn't have a great relationship with that person, it may be hard to understand your child's feelings.

Was this the death of someone who helped you with childcare? If you looked ahead in your crystal ball and saw this coming, hopefully you have already thought about how you will manage without this person. Of course, sometimes a death can occur very suddenly. It is always a good idea to have plan B. What is your plan B? This story might help you prepare.

Grandma was always there for all of us. She met the kids at the bus stop and fed them and helped with homework until I picked them up. She usually had dinner for us, so I did not have to go home and cook. No one knew she had a heart problem, so we were shocked when she died unexpectedly. We knew she was getting older, but we never expected she would be gone so suddenly. What will we do? I have no one else I can depend on. We are all so sad. My job only gives me three days off to figure this out.

***

If your ex experiences a loss like this one, it will give you a chance to shine and show everyone what a quality person you are. You can offer to help and in the time immediately following the death, make sure the child is at the appropriate place at the appropriate time, well groomed and dressed. (This can be a great help if shirts are wrinkled, hair needs cutting and dress shoes no longer fit.)Give the child small quiet toys for entertainment in case funeral services drag on. Whatever fusses and fights you have had, this is the time to put those aside. Be respectful by dressing your child appropriately. This is not about you, so whatever your feelings, keep your mouth shut.

Someone moves

It might be you or it might be the other side who moves. It might be just across town, or it might be out of town. It might be for a very good reason, as in this story.

I have been a medical computer programmer for several years. Last week, the school where I trained called and said there was a special graduate program in another city for people just like me. The school offered me a scholarship to train for twelve months, with free housing. This degree would mean I could become a manager and make a lot more money. How can I say no to that? I need to go.

***

Or it might be for a really lousy reason, as in the next story.

She has always hated her family, but she moved to their hometown just to keep me away. It is one thousand miles away. She doesn't have a job there. There is no college nearby for her to go to. When we were together, she refused to go visit there even for holidays. Now, to spite me, she left with no notice. I just want to be present in my child's life. I want him to have two parents, not just one. I will leave her alone if that is what she wants, but I intend to be there for my child.

***

Whatever the reason, moving raises tough issues. It may also raise legal issues, since almost every state has rules about moving more than one hundred miles away. These rules affect any court-ordered visitation. What are *your* state's laws about moving the child?

- **REFEREE'S RULE:** Most states require specific written notice from the parent with custody before that parent can move and take the child away. If written notice is given and the other parent does nothing, the parent can move. If there is a court order, it stays in place regardless of the move until a court changes or modifies the order.

- **PRACTICAL TIP:** Hire a lawyer to help you through this if the move is for a really good reason and far away.

- **TALKING TIP:** "We can work this out. I know this will be hard for all of us, but I have a really good opportunity and I must take it. This means we are moving to Nashville. Let's mediate how we want to handle visitation, so you still get the same amount of time you have always had. We can work out summer and holidays to make up for the other days. We can work this out."

- **LEGAL TIP:** Look up the law in your state. This is a high-risk issue, so hiring a lawyer may be money well spent.

The most important change of all (drum roll, please) is *you*

We have talked about the most likely change of events that will take place in the next five to ten years. But what about you? You are facing challenging circumstances, all the while trying to achieve what is best for your child. You have been constantly negotiating with the other parent and everyone else in the picture. Maybe you have had to make bold moves, like going to court to protect your child, or to make sure there is money to support your child's basic needs. Chances are, despite the difficulties, you are getting better at all of this. You are learning to be wise, tolerant, patient and strong.

Our conclusion: The most predictable and obvious change is *you*. You will grow, mature and learn to see the world through different eyes. When these change events take place, you will be ready.

CHAPTER NINE

What to Do about Who is the Dad
Paternity and DNA

Who is the mom? That is easy in the case of a birth mom. You know (boy, do you know!) you gave birth to the child and you are the mother.

For the dad, it can be much more complicated. Legally, if you are married to the mom, you are the legal father of the child, no matter what the DNA or deoxyribonucleic acid says.

What if you are *not* married to the mom? The possibilities are many and complex.

These are the primary options regarding paternity for unmarried parents:

- The easiest way to be the dad if the mom is not married to someone else is by *signing a form at the hospital when the baby is born*. This form is called a Voluntary Acknowledgement of Paternity, or VAP, and makes the dad the legal father of the child. The father's name (your name) is put on the birth certificate. What if he misses that chance?

- If dad did not sign the VAP at the time of the child's birth, he can still become the child's legal father. Some states allow *mom and dad to both go together to the Health Department, Office of Vital Records and sign the VAP together*. Every state has different locations.

- *Mom and dad can also go to Family Court, Juvenile Court or the Child Support office and file a petition* to establish him as the father. Here, you admit under oath you are the dad and sign by agreement. All parties must testify, or swear under oath. Usually, this includes a DNA test done on all of you, the dad, mom and child, which proves whether or not you are the father of the child.

All this looks pretty simple. When does it get complicated?

- Well, it gets complicated when a man is not willing to legitimate his child. The mother or the state (when child support is sought) undergo a process called establishment of paternity, in which *the mom goes to the family court in her state to add a man as the legal father of a child* and list his name on the child's birth certificate. DNA testing is required. A court must issue an order with findings that say he is the dad based on the DNA test. Often a paternity warrant is issued for the man's arrest in order to get him to cooperate.

- It gets complicated if the mother is still married to someone else. That man/husband is the legal father regardless of whether he is the biological father. His name will be listed on the birth certificate. *Parties must go to court to have his name removed as the father.*

When the mother is already married and the legal father is the mother's husband, the way to change that is the husband's name must be removed as the father first before another man can be added. A DNA test is required. The court order in this case must state the legal father's name is to be *removed* from the birth certificate. Then, as a result of the DNA evidence, another man's name is placed on the birth certificate as the father.

DNA test results with no court order will not make the man the legal father. To be the father, there must be a court order, VAP or marriage.

Establishment of paternity (that is, when you go to court to add a man as the legal father of a child and list his name on the child's birth certificate) has a few more twists and turns. A positive *court-ordered* DNA test is sufficient evidence to take a case to court to establish paternity, even if the man does not admit the child is his. If the man does not admit he is the father, even after a DNA test, a court must rule, based on the evidence of the *court-ordered* DNA test. At the end of the day, there must be a court order with DNA findings and a ruling that he is in fact the father of the child.

Disestablishment of paternity is when you go to court to remove the legal father from the child's birth certificate because the *legal* father is found not to be the child's *biological* father as a result of DNA testing.

By now, you should be getting an idea about the importance of DNA testing. It is a game-changer if there ever was one.

- **REFEREE'S RULE for Mom:** Always legitimate the child and have the correct father's name on the child's birth certificate. Either file a petition with the court and get a DNA test done or do the voluntary acknowledgement of paternity where the dad signs the paper by consent/agreement. If there is *any* chance at all another man might be the father, get a DNA test done immediately. The earlier you deal with any questions, the better it will be in the long run.

- **REFEREE'S RULE for Dad:** Confirm you are the father either with a court approved DNA test or a private DNA test. Even a mail order, motherless DNA test can let you know if you should follow up and do more. Remember, only the *court-ordered* DNA test can be used in court.

The power of DNA

Once upon a time, interested parties had to guess who the daddy was, based on who the mother had sex with, when they had sex and how much the child looked like the daddy in question. Since the early 1980's, DNA has become available, affordable and widely used in our legal system. It can tell you with 99.99% accuracy if a man is the child's biological father.

DNA testing, or paternity testing, is the scientific test of comparing the fifteen human genomes of DNA between a man, a mother and a child to determine if the man is the biological father. Cells are taken from the man, the mother and the child, either with a swab (inside of the cheek), blood sample, hair sample or for a possible parent who has died, a forensic sample. (For more information, go online and visit www.dna-geneticconnections.com)

DNA test results can *only* be wrong if:

- The wrong person is tested, resulting in a false negative. (It would have been positive if the right guy had been tested.)

- The father has an identical twin and the twin is tested.

- The father has had a blood transfusion within the past three months.

- The father has had a bone marrow or stem cell transplant recently.

DNA testing is 99.99% accurate otherwise and courts accept the official written DNA test results as sufficient proof of paternity.

That's it. It is THAT simple. Or, is it?

For DNA test results to be used as proof in court, they must first be court-ordered by a judge or authorized by the court's testing agency (child support agency) and be performed by a court- approved lab that can verify the chain of custody. That means identifying every location and every hand that has touched the sample from the moment it was taken from the parties to the time it comes back to court with the results.

Mail-order DNA testing is available, too, but it is only good for giving you a baseline idea of whether you should go forward with formal testing. If the test is positive and says you are the father, that is probably accurate. There is always the option of doing a DNA test and keeping the results secret, but can you keep a secret like this? Only you can decide, but secrets almost always have a way of being discovered.

Can you handle the truth? Do you really want to know?

DNA testing is magical. DNA testing is miraculous. DNA test results can put your mind at ease or ruin your life. The bottom line is DNA testing puts the truth—unquestionable, scientific proof of paternity—on the table, for better or worse. Yet it is not always easy to tell whether that information will be for better or worse. These stories show what can happen.

He wants to marry me. He assumes he is the dad. If I tell him there might be another guy, it will be all over. He will leave me. I was just on the rebound. That other guy didn't mean anything to me.

***

She says I'm the dad, but now she refuses to see me or allow me to see the child. Is it because I am not the real dad or because I hit her the last time we were together?

***

I signed the birth certificate at the hospital, but now I have doubts. I keep putting off doing anything about it. The kid is almost five and will start school soon.

***

We all agree there might be another guy who is the dad. We all agree to a test. Time to just do it.

***

We broke up for a month about nine months before the baby was born. I don't know who she was with then and I don't want to accuse her of something that will mess up what we have going. However, my family says I really need to be sure.

***

How do I do this?

Honesty is the best policy, but no one says it is easy. For example, how do you get a DNA test when you and the mother have been together and you know she will be very, very offended at the mere suggestion of DNA testing? How do you bring up getting a DNA test when you are happy together and everything is going great? Maybe you are the mother and only you know you had that one-night stand with your former high-school boyfriend the weekend you went back to your old hometown to visit your parents. Everything else is great, so why rock the boat? Are you being a little paranoid? Do you have reason to be?

- **REFEREE'S RULE:** Get the truth early. Find out for sure who the father of your child is, and do it the minute you have doubt. Do it in a way that is calm and respectful. Show the time frame of a break up, another date or a big party. Waiting and not resolving this issue can cause tension and drama for the rest of your life. It will lead to anxiety that can result in health problems. Do this before your child really knows what's going on.

- **PRACTICAL TIP:** The drug store test is a start, but it is not guaranteed accurate and cannot be used in court.

- **TALKING TIP:** "I know this is going to be hard, but it is the right thing to do."

- **LEGAL TIP:** Get a copy of the child's birth certificate and make sure it is correct.

Deciding what to do about paternity is an important consideration. Think carefully about where this will take you. Remember that once the information is out, there is no going back.

If you think you are not the father and think you might want DNA testing, this referee's advice is to do it now or not at all. Immediately.

I signed the birth certificate at the hospital, so I guess I am the dad. I didn't do a lot after the baby was born, though, and I never got close to the kid. She put me on child support, but it wasn't a lot. They took it out of my paycheck when I worked at a job, but since I have been working for myself I haven't paid it. I go by and see the kid occasionally. He is about to be ten and it occurred to me he doesn't look like anybody in my family. Hey, I think I'll get a DNA test. Also, they put a lien on my bank account for child support that I owe from last year.

***

This is such an important decision. It is way too important to decide after ten years you do not want to be this child's father. It also seems suspiciously tied to the child support. Waiting that long, not taking care of business when the child was young, not to mention it could be traumatic for the child—all of this makes a DNA test at this point unforgivable. It is always hard on a child for the man who is supposed to be his father to file a petition to NOT be his father. Waiting that long is just wrong.

It is worth saying again: Do it early or do not do it at all.

Here are the important technical terms you should know regarding paternity:

- **Chain of custody-** Proof that a specific medical person has had possession of the sample with the DNA evidence consistently and under secure conditions so someone else's DNA could not have been substituted.

- **Consent order of legitimation-** A legal court order that both mom and dad go to a court or the child support office in their community and sign agreeing the man is the biological father of the child.

- **Putative father-** A man who might be the biological father of a child, but is not married to the mother and no legal proceeding has found him to be the father.

- **Combined paternity index-** A ratio that shows the

probability of the tested man being the biological father in comparison to the probability of a random, unrelated man being the father.

- **Probability of paternity-** The percentage figure which either excludes the man as the father of the child or finds by 99.99% he is the father of the child. Always use a lab that goes to the one hundredth percentile.
- **Swab-** The sample taken by scraping the inside of the cheek of the father, mother and child, and which contains DNA for testing.

- **Blood draw-** The procedure by which a blood sample is drawn from the father, mother and child, and which contains DNA for testing. It is no better than the swab.

- **Hair sample-** Hair taken from one or all of the parties, which contains DNA for testing.

- **Forensic sample-** A sample taken from some part of the body of a possible parent who has died, which contains DNA for testing.

- **VAP** or **voluntary acknowledgement of paternity-** Also called VDP or voluntary declaration of paternity. A binding legal document where both parents agree the man is the biological father of a child. Parties waive a legal DNA test and the father agrees to support his child.

CHAPTER TEN
What to Do About Money
Child Support

Children cost money. Lots of money. They eat constantly and always seem to need more clothes, more books, more toys, more money for school. They get sick and need doctors. Children are relentless, twenty-four, seven obligations. The bottom line for this chapter is the money, and, more importantly, how do you get the other parent to pay a fair share of the enormous expense involved in raising a child?

When parents live separately but raise a child together, money issues can get complicated. Today, child support levels are controlled throughout the United States by computer formulas. Every state now has its own guideline that decides what the child support will be, based on information plugged into a computer.

State guidelines and the computer formulas only address children's costs. Property, cars, general expenses are not part of this for unmarried parents. For parents getting divorced, those couples also have houses, cars, property and stuff to divide. Not so for parents who never married. The turns and twists of child support do not happen in a vacuum. While the computer formula is pretty black and white, when it starts and what special credits are applied make a huge difference. This story covers every angle and mistake of a child support train wreck.

My wife and I lived in Cincinnati, Ohio and had two children. I had a girlfriend across the river in Covington, Kentucky. I lived my pretend life with my girlfriend, then went home to reality later. My girlfriend intentionally got pregnant because she thought I was rich...and single, and would marry her. I'm never going to divorce my wife. Heck, we were high school sweethearts. Our families are almost cousins and everything about our lives is together, not to mention I work for my father-in-law. Everything I own is really my wife's. When I wouldn't get a divorce, my girlfriend filed for child support in Kentucky, but I live in Ohio. I didn't think the Kentucky court would be able to make me pay. Man, was I ever wrong. The baby was conceived in Kentucky (my girlfriend had hotel receipts where I signed at the Kentucky hotel) but turns out the court could reach across the state line. Then, the court sent me notice by registered mail. When I did not show up, they ruled against me anyway and sent a garnishment or wage assignment to my job at my father-in-law's business.

When my wife found out, she kicked me out of the house. Her father fired me. I had no home, no job, no money. Nothing. By this time my girlfriend found out I was married and not rich. She would not speak to me. I haven't seen any of my kids in months. The baby is almost a year old now and I haven't seen him since the day he was born.

Now, my wife has filed for divorce. I couldn't afford a lawyer, and was too depressed and humiliated to show up for the divorce hearing, so I didn't go. She got the kids, the house, the car, and the court set child support on me. I don't even have a job! How can they do that? The final order said something about my last year's income and my earning ability and earning potential. That's crazy! How can I fix any of this?

***

What a disaster! He missed the boat at so many places. He will have to pick through this with a lawyer and try to get his life back on track. When you do the wrong thing so many times, you *will* get caught and you *will* have to pay.

- **REFEREE'S RULE:** Always go to court when you are supposed to, and if it is complicated, get a lawyer.

- **PRACTICAL TIP:** If you have more than one or two child

support orders for several children with different mothers or different guardians, your child support situation *will* become very complicated. If multiple states are involved, you can find yourself being garnished by multiple states for multiple mothers. *That* is complicated. The states expect *you*, the payor/parent/father to figure it out based on court orders and make sure everyone gets paid correctly in each state. If it is not done exactly right, *you* are the one who goes to jail. It may not sound fair, but that is the reality.

- **LEGAL TIP:** Child support is based upon computer-generated formulas that govern all child support calculations. The guidelines are different in every state. Go to your state's child support guidelines to figure out what you will pay.

First Step: How to get child support set.

If you want to *get* child support paid regularly, you can hire your own lawyer or you can go to your county's Child Support office. This is sometimes called the Title IV-D office, after the federal law that requires child support be paid. The child support office might be in a court, but usually it is run by a private company. Your state is required by federal law to have this office and collect the child support that is court ordered from the paying parent. Your state must provide a lawyer who will file for child support on behalf of the state. That means the state wants the child support collected and the state's lawyer works to collect the support, no matter what the parents say they want.

These state lawyers usually have a very large case load. If a case is simple, they can often get the support set so that within three months the child support office should begin sending a check to the parent with custody. *What is simple?* Simple is when everybody shows up on time with correct information about income and childcare. No one argues. No one disagrees.

If your case is *not simple*, it might take them much longer. In that case, you have the option to ditch your free state lawyer and hire your own private attorney. He or she can get the job done faster depending on how difficult your ex is. If your private attorney gets child support collected for you, the other parent has to pay the attorney. If your private attorney does not get any more support than what you have already been receiving, you will have to pay this attorney yourself.

What makes setting child support *not* simple or complicated? If no one can find your ex, or your ex works at a job that only pays cash, or your ex is hiding his income so no one can figure out how much he really makes, those are things that will cause it to take longer.

The bottom line is in order to get child support, you must file a petition unless the child support office has already filed it for you. You may be surprised to find the office has already filed it for you, when you did not even ask for it. How does that happen?

If you ever got any government money for your child or children such as food stamps, welfare and/or free medical care, you are already in the state's system and the child support office has already filed for you. When you signed up for these benefits, you signed up for the state to go after the child support and for your child to be in the child support system. This means the state will start this process automatically. They will begin everything for the parent who has custody of the child or children and will process everything through the system for you, whether you want it or not. At the same time, you can also be filing for support and the other parent can be filing to be put on child support.

To get child support paid, it is essential to get a court order. Otherwise all payments are voluntary gifts and can be stopped at any time. The paying parent does not get credit for voluntary gifts. This story shows gifts this parent will not get credit for.

After the baby was born I took her one hundred dollars every Saturday, well, most Saturdays. Then, we broke up and I stopped going. My sister started helping her by bringing her diapers, formula and clothes every few weeks. She would also pick up the baby and help out sometimes.

***

All of the payments of one hundred dollars will be considered gifts by the court. He will not be given credit for gifts of diapers, formula and clothing. This is her side of the story.

> *We never saw him unless he wanted sex. Then, he would drop by on a Saturday after he had been out drinking. He knew he better bring some child support, so he always had twenty or thirty dollars. When my rent or light bill was due, I had to call and beg for more money. Then, his sister would drop by and help me out. She gave me all of her kids' hand-me-down clothes. I knew I could call her, but he only came by when he wanted something.*

***

This story is typical of what happens if parents just handle the money informally. It is not the same as a predictable, monthly check. This is the reason child support should be paid through the system.

Second Step: How much is it going to be?

After the petition is filed, the case goes first to a child support counselor, who will try to get both sides to agree to a set amount. This is like mediation. The amount is set by the computer based on the information the state lawyer already has. However, when it starts and what credits are given for childcare and insurance can depend on receipts you have saved. How does that work? What does the computer want to know or already know? Income is the main item. The state already knows your reported income. IT IS A BAD THING TO LET THE GOVERNMENT PUT YOU ON CHILD SUPPORT RATHER THAN DOING IT YOURSELF IN A TIMELY FASHION. Jump ahead of this parade and get it together for the good of everyone.

You should definitely do your own calculations to make sure you agree with the computer and online tools make that task easier than it once was. Every state has a free online worksheet and by going to your state's CHILD SUPPORT website, you can find a sample to use. Sometimes this is called a child-support calculator. (You can just Google "child support worksheet" for your state, then look for the sample.) After you plug in the numbers, you will know what the counselor is expecting. Is it correct? Is there anything else you want to tell the counselor? Did they leave out something, such as your visitation and daycare contributions? If you do not agree with the counselor, you will go before a judge. He or she will look at the numbers, the guidelines, the worksheet and decide the final numbers.

So, what are the numbers that are plugged into the computer worksheet? The following are the numbers that make a real difference:

- How much time do you spend with your child? That is called parenting time and is measured in actual twenty-four hour day/night blocks.

- What is the cost of the daycare/afterschool/babysitter the custodial parent needs in order to go to work? Who pays it? This is only for childcare costs during work hours, not necessarily private school costs.

- Who pays for health insurance and how much is it?

- Are there any really high medical costs?

- What other children live in each parent's home? Other children in the home or out of the home do count.

- How much do you *actually* pay in child support for other children?

A few things might matter a little, depending on the judge:

- Family contributions

- School expenses

- Private school tuition, if both parents signed the private school contract

- Recurring medical bills that are not large

- Reason for no visitation (What if the parent with custody has interfered?)

- Extracurricular activities of the child, which cost extra and are paid by one parent

How much money both parents make is the first and most important number. In figuring out income, the computer looks at both parents' present income. However, if there is no accurate present income, what really matters next is:

- His/her past income

- His/her ability to earn

- His/her education

- His/her reason for a decrease in income

- His/her reason for changing employment

The following do not matter at all in calculating child support:

- House note/car note

- Bankruptcy

- Debt

- Expenses

- Girlfriend/boyfriend/spouse's income

- Lame reason for no visitation

- Grandparents' visitation, *unless* you show dad or mom joined and participated in the visits, thus adding to the parent's visitation time.

This is a lot of information, so you may want to use the workbook in the back to pull it all together. These questions, along with answer space are at Appendix F, "What to do About Money" for you to print, or at www.singleparentreferee.com.)

- **REFEREE'S RULE:** If you are paying the other parent direct money on a regular basis, pay it through the system, that is, through the court, or you will not get credit for any of your payments.

- **PRACTICAL TIP:** Keep your documents in one file or one box so you do not lose things. Keep everything.

- **TALKING TIP:** "I think our child support should be paid through the system."

- **LEGAL TIP:** This can get ugly quick. If you have any suspicion your child might be getting government aid, you should go to the child support department in your area and *put yourself on child support* before they come and get you. You can take charge of this before it takes charge of you. That keeps the order in a court near you. It gets something started so you will not be surprised when you are summoned to court. It will also keep you from getting behind in the beginning.

Third Step: What if there is a problem?

Child support problems generally boil down to one of two things:

1. The parents disagree on the amount of child support. Not surprisingly, the parent who is paying child support thinks it is too much and the parent receiving child support thinks it is not enough.

2. The paying parent tries to avoid his or her child support obligation by moving out of state, hiding assets and other maneuvers. Sometimes, though, the parent cannot pay because of job loss or other factors.

When parents disagree about the amount of child support

In the case of parents disagreeing about the amount of child support, often there is little they can do to change it. The amount depends on the formula of the child support guidelines in the state in which the child lives.

However, if the amount is ridiculously low because the income numbers the state uses are not correct, you can appeal the child support amount in court. This is probably the best option if you suspect the paying parent is hiding money in order to lessen his or her child support. You will need to get documentation, hire a lawyer and perhaps even hire a detective to prove the other parent's income is being understated to the judge.

Remember all that information we asked you to pull together in the earlier chapters? Now you can see why it is a good idea to collect information about income and credit cards and bank accounts early. Then, you might not need the detective. If you use this workbook, your Appendix A, B and D will have it all. YOUR CALL.

If you are the one who is thinking about trying to fake your income to get lower child support, be forewarned. You can go to prison for lying in court, and you can get hit with a significantly higher child support than you would otherwise pay. A decrease in child support is usually successful only when there is a significant increase in parenting time spent with the child or a valid, believable decrease in income through no fault of the paying parent.

Keep in mind each state has different laws regarding calculation of child support and you should look them up for your own state. Every state uses a worksheet, often called a calculator, which is available for free on line. You will be able to plug in the numbers discussed above and see what the amount of child support is likely to be. Go to your state's child support website. Put in "child support calculator." This is the same thing as the sample worksheet. Fill in the blanks.

Here are the points on which states are most likely to be *different,* so it is worth your time to find out what the law is in *your* state and/or the state where your child lives:

Retroactive child support. This is what you should have paid in the past. The court can order you to pay it in a lump sum or add it as part of the monthly payment on top of the regular child support. Some states set retroactive support back to birth, while other states set retroactive support back two years or to the date the petition was originally filed.

- Most states do not consider the personal expenses of the non-custodial parent.

- Virtually all states consider visitation/parenting time in calculating child support.

- Some states add lines for childcare, private school tuition, extracurricular activities, etc. Some states will not consider those expenses.

- Most states end child support at age eighteen. Others order child support be paid until the child turns twenty-one.

Although states differ on lots of little points, they all agree about one thing: If a child has ever received government assistance, the parent who does not have custody will pay. The different states now talk to each other and their computers keep up with the trail. The mother is now on a five-year limit for receiving government assistance, but the other parent will have to pay child support until the child is eighteen, or twenty-one, depending on the state.

Once again, any child who is enrolled for any kind of government assistance in any state in the United States is automatically placed in the system for child support enforcement, whether the custodian (mom, dad, guardian) wants it or not. This includes medical care, food assistance, welfare, government assisted housing assistance, and so on. Government payments for the birth of a child also place the child in the system for child support to be collected by the state.

Conversely, if no government assistance is ever requested, government child support departments do *not* get involved unless requested by one of the parents. Under those circumstances, you must go to the child support office and ask for child support. Or not.

When a parent tries to avoid paying child support

You can run, but you cannot hide. The law in this area has toughened up considerably in recent years and computer technology makes it possible and easy for states to work together to track down deadbeat dads and moms.

The government has many tricks up its sleeve when it comes to collecting child support. If you go to another state, the child support office in your child's state will find you. If you do not pay, the government can have the amount taken out of your paycheck. What happens when you work for a family business that does not withhold and send in child support from your paycheck? The government can take action against the business that can result in a tax intercept, bank lien, property lien or license revocation.

The Uniform Interstate Family Support Act (UIFSA) gives states the right to collect child support from a parent who does not live in their state. These laws are long and complicated, so you need a lawyer if you are involved in a child support case involving multiple states. If the alleged father used to live with the child in that state, or sent the child to that state to live, or had sexual intercourse in that state resulting in the child's conception and birth, all of these can allow a court in that state to claim the right to set child support and collect it, even when the father does not live in that state.

That is not all. There is another entire list of ways a non-custodial parent can be ordered to pay child support by and in a state where he or she does not live. You have to hire a lawyer for all those situations. To learn more, go to http://www.acf.hhs.gov/programs/cse/fct/uifsahb.htm.

Here are some ways in which the government can collect child support from you whether you want them to or not.

Income withholding is when the child support ordered by the court, plus any amount for arrears or medical bills, is taken directly out of that parent's paycheck and sent to a state child support office. This office then sends the money to the custodial parent, but takes out a pay back amount to the government.

Income withholding, also called wage assignment or garnishment, is ordered by the original court that sets the child support. Then, the child support office sends a letter by regular mail to that parent's employer.

When employers receive this withholding order, they must treat it as a court order, inform the employee by giving him or her a copy of the order immediately and pay the money as directed. This income withholding order may only be stopped when the employer gets another order from the same court stating the order has been changed.

- **REFEREE'S RULE:** Never go cheap about your child. Living within your means is different from being cheap.

- **PRACTICAL TIP:** Always study your child support statements and make sure they are accurate. If there is a problem, deal with it immediately.

- **TALKING TIP:** "We do not discuss our money issues in front of our child."

- **LEGAL TIP:** When you change jobs, inform the child support office and fill out the form to change the income assignment.

FREQUENTLY ASKED QUESTIONS ABOUT CHILD SUPPORT

When I was a magistrate judge, the following were always questions people would ask.

What if *other* children in the household get benefits? That will still cause the entire household to be in the system and all fathers or parents not living in the household will be put on child support.

What interest is charged on arrearages? Some states charge as much as 12%, but that changes state by state.

How do you figure income? Income is based on an IRS report or W-2 from prior year, recent pay stub with year-to-date pay or a statement of hourly rate from the employer.

What can happen without proof of income? Support will be set based on presumptive income or a good guess looking at the following:
1) The median income of persons in your state.
2) The minimum wage if you have never made more.
3) The income of a person typical of your earning ability.

What happens if you are unemployed? The court will ask if:
1) you get unemployment payments.
2) you quit.
3) you got fired.

What does it mean to be underemployed? How does that affect child support? Working for a fast-food restaurant as a cook with a college degree is considered underemployed. Most courts look at earning ability and earning history.

What bank accounts are available for child support? All of them.

What credit applications are significant? Applications for car or house loans. These loan applications show what you told a bank about how much money you made in order to get the loan. If that loan application is not true, you either committed bank fraud or perjury. You'd better have a really good reason for it to not be correct.

What payments are regularly made to credit cards every month? The amount of the payments and the credit card statement matter since this shows how much cash a person has access to every month.

Can you get lower child support for coaching sports events? No.

Can you get lower child support for picking up from school every day? Maybe.

Can you get lower child support if your family member provides childcare? Sometimes.

Can you get lower child support if you pay for childcare? Yes.

Can I pay my sister, mom, neighbor for childcare? It depends if they run a licensed day care.

What does the law consider to be childcare? Official, licensed daycare or after school program.

Do I have to pay for private school tuition? Depends on who registered the child and signed the contract, as well as whether both parents agreed to register the child and pay the cost.

CHAPTER ELEVEN
What to Do About Parenting Time
Parenting Time, AKA Visitation

"Come on over any time." Uh, no. Anyone who has been there can tell you it really does not work that way. Visiting any time, on a drop-in basis, will always cause problems. Without exception. Everyone needs a parenting plan. There needs to be an understanding, a schedule and some rules. We talked about the problems of visitation or parenting time in Chapter Three. Now come the solutions.

You may recall parenting time/visitation often becomes the battleground for power struggles and there is almost always conflict. For those reasons, parenting time/visitation must be handled with as much discipline and patience as you can muster. How you handle conflict will define how well parenting time/visitation goes and that will define how well everything else will go. It is worth the effort to learn how to disagree nicely and resolve the issues at hand. Figure out how to do this and you will have a good life. If you spend your time overreacting, being defensive or saying ugly things to the other parent, you will regret and dread every encounter you have with that person. That can be pretty depressing if you consider that seeing that person is an inevitable part of your life as long as you have a child together.

> *I had filed for court-ordered parenting time with my child because every time the mom got angry with me she would stop our agreed visitation. This was her way of controlling me. She was always jerking me around, messing with my mind. I'm a firefighter and when I am off work I want to be able to spend time with my child. In this job, when I am at work I can't visit at all. My schedule rotates and changes every week. The mom*

now says she does not want the court's involvement and we can work it out. I told the judge, "Your Honor, when there is no clear understanding there will always be a misunderstanding." No truer words were ever spoken.

***

Setting parenting time is often a major legal issue, so here we get into the nitty gritty of how our legal system handles it. Putting together an official parenting plan that sets out the specifics of visitation is the best way to go. The parenting plan spells out the scheduled time for everything, then makes it a court order that is difficult to change. Both sides must follow the plan.

- **PRACTICAL TIP: Make sure you know what a parenting plan is. A good example can be found at www.tsc.state.tn.us/sites/default/.../parenting plan. It may not fit every state, but it is a start.**

There are four steps to dealing with parenting time/visitation:

- First, file a petition for parenting time/visitation to be set. This starts the process.

- Second, mediate the parenting time/visitation plan and get a permanent parenting plan. Know what you want.

- Third, go to court with the mediated agreement, which then becomes a court order.

- Fourth, follow the order. Do not mess up the plan.

In many states, you must put together a *parenting plan* as part of mediation. That is where you help make the rules that *you* can follow. This is the only way to sensibly work out your plan. It can be a disaster if you try to do it in the courtroom, in front of the judge. After the petty arguing and bickering gets to a certain point, the judge will become impatient to clear the matter away, especially if there are more cases after yours. He or she could likely just set any plan without considering all of the small detail such as pick-ups, drop-offs, office schedules and family help (or lack of help).

> *I asked the judge for every other weekend from Friday immediately after school until Monday morning. Problem is, I hadn't asked my boss if I could get off early every other Friday and she wouldn't change my schedule. So, when I could not follow the order and I was always late, the other parent got mad, my child got upset, the school made a big deal out of it and when we went back to court to change it, I had to pay all the court costs and lawyer expenses for both sides.*

The fifty states have fifty variations regarding the laws about visitation and parenting time. However, there is always a theme of encouraging as much parenting time as possible with both parents. In fact, the trend in most states is toward encouraging equal parenting time, especially involvement with fathers.

Why mediation is best for getting the parenting time/visitation schedule you want.

If you want to get what is best for your schedule and in the best interest of your child, mediate it. *Do not go to trial over parenting time/visitation if you can possibly avoid it*. To explain why I offer this warning, I will share with you what goes on behind the scenes in a court. The bottom line about visitation is judges *hate,* absolutely *hate* long trials involving parenting time/visitation. When I worked as a judicial referee, the cases for visitation were all grouped together on two separate days. The court tradition was the newest judge had to hear those dockets because no one else wanted these cases. It was a promotion to finally be senior enough in the job to never have to listen to two people bicker, argue and snipe at each other about visitation and parenting time. It brings out the worst in the parents. Then, the lawyers chime in, bickering over the smallest points just to show their client they are working hard for them.

Because judges hate these cases so much, they are impatient and irritable while listening to the division of time and pettiness that goes with it. You can end up with a schedule that does not work. Thus, to really get what is good for your schedule and for your child, do not go to trial on visitation. Mediating this conflict is absolutely the best way to handle it. Sit down with a trained, neutral mediator and take out your calendar, your schedule and your watch. Knock out the issues day by day, week by week, holiday by holiday.

Standard versus custom designed parenting time/visitation plans

The standard is for the mother to be the primary residential parent and the father to have every first, third and fifth weekends, from six pm on Friday to six pm on Sunday, plus one week at Christmas, two weeks in the summer and alternating other holidays.

Everything else is custom designed. For parents who want a fifty/fifty arrangement, some courts will allow alternating weeks when both parents live in the same school district and it is not too disruptive. Sometimes courts will allow four days one week and three days the next week to give each parent equal time. Being creative depends on what is good for your child. How much moving around is stable for your child? Think about this story.

> *It wasn't an ugly split. We just broke up. So, I told him he could visit our daughter any time he wanted. Sometimes after work, he would want to swing by and read her a story and tuck her in. I understood. It was perfectly natural. He's a great dad and she adores her daddy. Then, I started dating. It was so awkward for him to drop in when I had a date or when she and I had other plans. He did not want to get back together, but when he showed up and I was already in my PJs, he would want to have sex. He just wanted all the benefits with none of the responsibility. That made me mad. So, I just wouldn't go to the door if I wasn't dressed. Well, he still had a key to my house, so he let himself in and just walked right back to her bedroom. It scared me to death, then it made me angry. I flew off at him. I cut off all of his parenting time and threatened to call the police if he ever came back.*

***

- **REFEREE'S RULE:** How you handle conflict will define everything else. Learn how to disagree nicely and resolve the issue and you will have a good life. Spend your time over-reacting, being defensive, saying snide, ugly things and you will regret and dread every encounter. Visitation will take the first hit.

- **PRACTICAL TIP:** If you cannot say something nice at a visitation exchange, do not say anything at all. Do most of your communication by text message and e-mail. Do not ever push SEND when you are mad and have said something you will regret.

- **TALKING TIP:** "I respect you as a parent and I know we have gotten along well in the past. For the kids' sake, let's put together a visitation plan so we can get along well in the future."

- **LEGAL TIP:** This is where mediation is worth every penny. It should also be used when a grandparent wants to visit and there is conflict.

The details of parenting time/visitation: Who, what, when, where and how.

These are questions you should ask and answers you are entitled to when it comes to your child having parenting time with the other side.

Again, it is time for workbook mode. Question and answer space are also in Appendix G or at www.singleparentreferee.com.

1. Who will the child actually visit? In whose house? It is okay and sometimes better when a child visits grandparents, aunts, uncles or other siblings, as well as the other parent. As long as the environment is good, do not complain when dad's or mom's parents handle most of the visitation, especially when parents are very young, irresponsible or work long hours.

Who will be in charge and supervising? Who else will be there, such as the bully cousin or felon uncle? The dope smoking aunt? The pervert in-law? *You* are entitled to know.

2. You are entitled to know what your child will be doing. That is particularly true when the other parent is at work all day and the child will be there for two weeks, or a month or summer extended visitation. You are entitled to know what activities will be maintained, what activities will be added, what day camp is provided and what overnight camp the child is going to attend.

3. You are entitled to know who the neighbors and friends are, which overnight friends visit. Will your child be near water? (It is always a good idea to teach your child to swim at a young age so water is not so much of a danger.)

4. When will the child go and when will the child return to you? A weekend visit is typically six pm Friday to six pm Sunday, but it can change depending upon everyone's work schedule. When is school out? What time is work over? How much travel time is involved? Picking up a child from school avoids conflict between the parents. What happens on school holidays? Ask.

5. How will transportation be handled?
You should have an address. Going out of town or on vacation should be allowed, but parents should know where the child is going and how the child is getting there. When separated parents live in different towns, the options for transportation usually are:

- Meet halfway.

- One parent drives the pick-up trip and the other parent drives the return trip.

- Meet at a neutral place that might not be halfway.

- Pick up at home.

- Fly as an unaccompanied minor.

- Travel with another person.

6. Parents have the right to regular phone contact and private communication by e-mail or text when their child is staying with the other parent. While it is the role of a responsible parent to be vigilant about what goes on during visits with the other side, you should not let your imagination run wild. For some parents, having their child away from home is agonizing and they are sure there will be an accident or terrible experience. Face what you are afraid of. List the possibilities: Lack of safety, neglect, violence, irresponsible behavior, lack of control, accidents. You may realize the chances of these scenarios actually happening are fairly small. The real problems most parents face involve a bad attitude and disorganization.

My teenager comes home from visits with the other parent in a rude, disrespectful mood. He starts complaining or arguing with me the minute he walks in the door. Nothing I do is right and every comment I make leads to World War Three. If I just stay out of the way for the rest of the day, ask no questions and give no orders, things seem to settle down. When I start pushing on homework, chores, and such, it gets worse. If I ask anything about the weekend, he is really ugly.

***

Visitation causes so much stress and drama. He or she often cancels the visit at the last minute. He is late or cuts the visit short. He talks about his other kids a lot and their big trips and successes. He talks about me and questions our child a lot. Everything about it is not quite right. He asks what we spend money on and pumps and prods about who I am with and what I buy. It is all so creepy. The visitation causes so much resentment.

***

Our child really does not like going to her house. It is always a mess. That's why I got custody, because she is a hoarder and the place is a disaster and always chaotic. She has stacks and stacks of junk everywhere. Our child does not even have a bed but has to clear off the sofa to find a place to sleep. I'm going to give him a cell phone with a good camera to take pictures, then we are taking that to the judge. If we go to court, I'll ask the court to only allow her to come to his events, take him out to eat after that and visit him on Sunday afternoons at the library, church or a movie. That's all until she gets some help.

***

They'll go to his house for Christmas Eve. He'll have cereal, maybe milk. It will not be an event of any kind. No presents, no celebration, nothing that involves any planning or trouble. He is the laziest human on the face of the planet. I say nothing bad about him to my child because someday she will know the difference, she will know the truth, but she still needs to love him because he is her father. If I talk badly about him, in a strange way she will be mad at me for what he is not. She will blame me for his weaknesses…for not fixing him. I cannot be part of anything with his life. She is safe with him, though. He is a handy baby-sitter.

***

What happens when visitation is a potential nightmare?

My daddy has a new girlfriend who has moved into his apartment. Every weekend her teenage son comes for her visitation with him. He smokes funny little cigarettes, watches TV shows where people don't have their clothes on and always wants to wrestle and push me around.

***

This is a formula for disaster. Step in.

What happens when visitation is a control thing?

She/he uses visitation to string me along. She is thirty minutes to an hour late just so she can control what I am doing and how my visits will begin. She is not working late, she just runs errands or does not leave her house on time. She can't control

140

anything else, but she manipulates the visits. She doesn't send extra clothes, or she sends old shoes that are too small. She schedules his dentist appointment in the middle of my visits.

***

- **REFEREE'S RULE:** Picking up a child from school or a grandparent's house usually reduces conflict because you will not see the other parent. Always honor the agreed times.

- **PRACTICAL TIP:** Try to avoid shipping clothes back and forth. Each parent should keep their own set of weekend clothes and school clothes. Leaving a belt or socks somewhere is not worth a big fight. Also, buy socks by the dozen.

- **TALKING TIP:** "I want to call our child once a day when he or she is at your house. What would be a good time?"

- **LEGAL TIP:** Make sure your visitation order sets out the time and place of pick-up and drop-off. Spell out what happens when there is no school. Spell out who gets which holidays, especially Monday holidays when kids are out of school.

The visitation story can have a happy ending. This final story represents the dream parenting time or visitation situation for young children. As you will see, it takes a lot of work on the part of the parents to make this dream come true. This is the best visitation ever for young children and is what you should try to make happen for your child.

Once upon a time, a little girl lived with her mommy and visited her daddy. In one house she had her very own room and in the other house, she shared a room with an older sister. In both houses, she had a cute little chest that had been unpainted when they got it. Her sister got one, too. They put stickers on the chests and painted each one in their favorite colors. Mommy and Daddy helped and that was fun, but everything was her idea. This chest was for all of the special treasures she had that were too fragile or special to share. This chest was all hers. It was where she could put things every time she left and the chest full of treasures would be safe and protected. That was the rule and it was never broken. Ever.

In both houses, she had sheets and blanket with her favorite cartoon character. Her bed looked just the same at both houses. At both houses, she also had a special lovey to sleep with: Teddy the brown bear at mommy's house, and Pinky the pink raccoon at daddy's house. When she was gone overnight, each animal got to play in the special chest with her other special things until she came back. No one ever took them out of the chest or bothered these special animals. Ever.

At both houses, she had special pink cereal bowls that were just alike. She felt so good eating out of these same plastic bowls in the morning regardless of which house. She had pajamas, her tooth brush, jeans, shoes and some t-shirts at both houses. She never had to pack a suitcase to go to the other house. She even had a coat and boots at each house. Some were hand-me-downs from big sister, but she loved her sister's clothes.

It was her job to keep up with her school stuff, because both mom and dad told her she must learn to be responsible. That part was kind of hard, but she soon learned to remember her things.

Her schedule and her list of rules were always on the refrigerator door at her mom's house, and on the closet door at her dad's house. It was the same list, except at her dad's house, she had to feed the dog.

She is a happy little girl. She always knows where her stuff is. She always knows what's up and what's down. No surprises. She is never afraid that everything will be crazy or mom and dad will be angry. She will live happily ever after.

***

A word about grandparent visitation before we move on

The laws for grandparents vary from state to state. Be prepared for there to be no mandated grandparent visitation unless a parent dies. Some courts will order it when the grandparents have been the primary custodian of the child for many years.

If you have a great relationship with your child's grandparents and they are genuinely helpful to you in raising your child, thank your lucky stars. If these relationships are not so positive, you will need to be smart about managing them. They can help and you can make it work. Whatever that relationship is like, you must consider when grandparents get to visit or in some cases, when they get custody.

How do you do this? Every state has different laws about grandparent rights. If the child and parents live in another state, it is almost impossible to have court-ordered grandparent visitation. Grandparents get custody either by agreement of the parents or when the children are about to go into custody of the state.

- **REFEREE'S RULE:** Grandparent relationships can be very complicated. There is usually a combination of history, mistrust, anger, frustration and disappointment. Blood is always thicker than water.

- **PRACTICAL TIP:** If they are willing, let grandparents be your number one babysitter. Do not take advantage of them.

- **TALKING TIP:** "On Friday nights I can really make some extra money if I can work overtime without stressing about childcare. That is the one night of the week when I really need help with child care. Would it be possible for you all to help that night?"

- **LEGAL TIP:** Every state is different on grandparent visitation. Look it up.

When the other parent and grandparents do not want to visit, it can be complicated. Sometimes it is a relief and keeps down the drama.

Other times it becomes a source of real pain and disappointment. Help your child to not feel rejected. Make this a good thing. No hassles, no complications, no abuse, no ugly attitude.

Perhaps you can imply his visits are loose with no specific schedule. If your child is a teen, she might prefer to stay home near her friends. Try to make the absence normal. Treat it like you would a great uncle in Alaska. Occasionally, someone might discuss him, but not often and not with any emotional attachment.

CHAPTER TWELVE

What to Do About Custody AKA Primary Residential Parent

Parents might be fine with going to court over visitation issues, but everyone should be reluctant to do so over custody and for good reason. Custody is a much bigger and more serious fight and, if you are considering taking sole custody of your child, not one to undertake lightly. A custody battle in court can take you places you do not want to go. Without hardcore proof, custody fights can be unpredictable.

Mom starts out first, usually

In most states, the birth mother is presumed to be the legal custodian of a child born to a couple who are not married. In order to get joint custody, where parents share custody (and this is becoming the norm more and more), there must be a court order. This would usually happen when the child is legitimated by the court. At the legitimation/paternity hearing, if the parents both agree to joint custody, most courts will approve it. Joint custody is also called shared parenting or collaborative parenting. The concept is both parents will have equal involvement with their child. All states and most courts have rules and procedures that differ on this. Find out what your court's local rules are before you go in.

> *I've got two older kids in middle school. This baby was such a surprise. The dad has more time and patience. His mom is willing to help a lot. We should have joint custody, but he should be the primary residential parent.*

***

- **LEGAL TIP:** The primary residential guardian is the parent who usually makes most of the decisions. This is where the child spends most of his or her time. This is the first parent called when the child is sick at school.

- **LEGAL TIP:** If parents voluntarily agree to a change of custody to someone else such as grandparents, that parent will later have an easier time getting their child returned to them if this is a voluntary placement rather than if the parent loses custody of the child for reasons of neglect, dependency, abuse or abandonment.

Courts start out presuming biological parents are best for children. Next, if the parents are not available, courts presume family members are best. However, the best interest of the child is the primary test in most states. Some states, however, require a finding in court that a parent is unfit in order for that biological parent to have custody taken away. Proving a parent to be unfit is much harder than showing it is in the child's best interest to be with someone else.

It is much more involved if someone is seeking sole custody, that is, putting the child under the control of one person. For the father, grandparents, aunts, uncles or other relatives to get sole custody of a child, there must be a hearing and a court order.

Filing a legal petition for sole custody of a child is *not* something you do lightly. It is such a serious matter that parents' rights are protected by the court. You need a better reason than wanting to get even with the other parent. You do this because the other parent is physically incapacitated or is a totally irresponsible parent, putting the child at risk of serious harm. You must be specific about what harm could occur.

Perhaps the parent is addicted to drugs, going to prison, allowing your child to have contact with an abuser, not getting your child necessary medical care or getting inappropriate medical care. Then, you have reason to file for sole custody. You must specifically state the risk and the harm. Never assume a court knows what you are talking about.

Sole custody hearings almost always require an attorney. On rare occasions, when both sides are in total agreement, willing to go to court together, willing to sign the petition together and show up before a judge together, only then does a custody hearing not require lawyers. Without that level of agreement, filing for sole custody of a child usually results in an investigation by the Department of Children's Services, *and* the appointment of a guardian ad litem (GAL, or attorney for the child), *and* the appointment by the state of an attorney for the parent losing custody. All state laws are different, but they tend to agree on this point: In order to remove a child from the legal custody of a biological or adoptive parent, someone must give testimony in court that the parent is unfit, unwilling or unable to care for the child. In other words, there must be a live witness willing to go to court and swear or affirm before the court that one of those conditions exists.

- **REFEREE'S RULE:** Getting joint custody is usually a good thing if two parents can work together. Taking a child away from a parent is the most serious action you can take.

- **PRACTICAL TIP:** There is always a possibility of court action over custody or visitation. That is the reason to keep your notes, your calendar and answer the questions that are part of this book.

- **TALKING TIP:** "I think I am going to hire a lawyer."

- **LEGAL TIP:** Get certified copies of all court orders. Also, get copies of any other legal documents that might come in handy down the road.

Her wonderful, beautiful, intelligent mother was in a terrible car accident when our daughter was only four years old. We all pitched in to help, but burns rendered her unable to ever use her hands and the head injury messed up her short-term memory. She never left the nursing home but she never forgot her little girl. She wanted to see her every day but could not remember if she had seen her the day before. As she aged in the nursing home, she became more and more agitated by things and less rational. Going into a courtroom would have been impossible for her. The social workers were great. The nurses were terrific. It was all so sad. I had no choice but to ask for sole custody.

***

We lived together and had joint custody of two great kids. He smoked a little marijuana, then used pills to stay awake when he worked at night. He was a good dad. He was always good to us. Then, after his mom died, he added a few hits of cocaine. The kids were never around, they were teenagers by then and I thought he had it under control. Then he lost his job, but started living better. He bought a new car, paid for some expensive stuff, got lots of bling. I was curious, but I didn't ask. Then it came down. A big drug bust and he was involved. Cops searched our house, too. The kids saw it all and were horrified. The landlord made us move. We spent all our money on his legal fees, and he won't even be up for parole for five years. I've got to hold it together, but none of us is doing very well. I had to get sole custody of the kids so I could be in charge of the decisions.

***

I needed a sitter because I was working two jobs. I could not possibly afford childcare on my salary. Mom had been there for us and she was willing to help. She lived nearby and had a nice house. My dad had died when I was in high school and much later she married a retiree. As the girls have gotten older they have started telling me creepy things. He walks out of the bathroom naked and pretends to be surprised they are there. He asks them questions about their bodies when my mother is not in the room. He showed the older one pictures of naked men. Where is this going? Who should I tell? Nothing has happened. Their dad would go ballistic. He would file for custody if something happened. I've got to talk with someone to try and stop this before it gets really bad. I've got to do something now.

***

- **REFEREE'S RULE:** Sometimes life deals us a really bad blow. Put together a support network first. Get a plan. When you see the issues you face are not going to be cleared up soon, get connected to someone who can help you.

-

- **PRACTICAL TIP:** Have a plan. Do not act without thinking through all of the possibilities of where your actions could lead you. Have a plan for every side road. Write down all of your options.

- **TALKING TIP:** "We have some issues to discuss that are going to lead to some changes. Let us work out a plan together."

- **LEGAL TIP:** File the papers in court for custody as soon as you realize children are at risk of harm or major change will ultimately happen. Dragging it out does not improve things. Get ready to move forward.

Last, what do courts consider in a custody hearing?
- All available family

- Child's relationship with the family or the one who wants custody

- That person's track record as a parent

- The physical and mental health of the parties

- Ability to support the child

- Motive for wanting custody

- Sex and age of child, and of parties seeking custody

- Home environment based upon social worker's home study

- The child's preference, if he or she is mature

- Report of the guardian ad litem, GAL, (the court-appointed attorney for the child). Some courts also have a court appointed special advocate, CASA, to help the court evaluate everything. Remember, with children, everything changes when they become teenagers.

Question and answer space is in Appendix H and at www.singleparentreferee.com.

We had all been one big, happy family. His, hers and ours. Four kids total. Then my daughter, who was the oldest, decided she wanted to go live with her dad when she was fifteen. This really hurt our feelings. She thought life with him would be so much better, so much freer and so much happier. We had no idea she was unhappy. My husband was afraid she would get into so much trouble in the school near her dad, we fought the decision. That made it worse. She did get into trouble, then she wanted to come back to us. By then, my husband was afraid her issues would rub off on our other kids. He did not want her back. I did not know what to do.

***

Teenagers always think the grass is greener somewhere else. It is part of their mental preparation for moving away and being adults. However, their immature judgment often causes them to make choices that are clearly not in their best interest. When teenagers have a choice of one parent over another, they often choose something new and different or something easy and lenient. New and different is often the parent who has not been there. It is always a blow to the parent who was up in the night with this child as a baby, who was at the emergency room when this child was sick, who sacrificed to pay for gifts and trips. This parent often feels abandoned and rejected when the child wants to try out the other side. When I sat as a judicial referee, I felt so bad for parents who were in court because the teenager had declared a desire to live somewhere else. I could perfectly understand the resentment they felt.

Often, parents insist on holding on to the teen only to find themselves put through pure hell with a resentful, ungrateful, difficult teenager. No wonder raising a teenager seems like such a thankless job sometimes.

- **REFEREE'S RULE:** No good deed goes unpunished.

- **PRACTICAL TIP:** Get ready for your heart to be broken.

- **TALKING TIP:** "I will always love you, but I might not always be here."

- **LEGAL TIP:** Ask for a guardian ad litem (GAL) to be appointed for your teen.

CHAPTER THIRTEEN

What to Do About the Rest of Your Life
Finally

Finally, you think your parenting job will be over. You think when your child is eighteen you will not have to deal with issues about your ex and your child. You will never have to see your ex again.

Wrong.

Having children is a lifelong commitment. You might not provide them with money after a certain age and you hope you do not have them under your roof forever. You will always be thinking, worrying and anxious for your children and their well-being, though. Because of that, for better or worse, you will always be tied to the other parent.

It does not end when your child is eighteen, and it does not end at age twenty-one or thirty. There will be weddings and funerals, grandchildren and great-grandchildren. There will be graduations and many, many birthdays. Hopefully, they will be happy birthdays. Will you pout and sulk and play the victim at all of those events, or will you rise above it all and be the generous, favorite person whom everyone loves because you are *so much fun*? At the very least, you should make it your business *never* to be the person who is ruining the fun for your child and everyone else. Always be pleasant and positive. Re-read Chapter Seven, "Fake It," on a regular basis and certainly before every major occasion.

If you can get and keep a positive attitude, there will be many rewards for all the hard work it took to get there. The key is to not get your feelings hurt easily. If you are always easily wounded, others have to treat you with kid gloves. They will avoid you. They will not invite you to events because you are too sensitive and unpleasant. Thus, be the parent who is generous with holidays. Be the parent who shares parenting time graciously, because when you willingly allow them to go, your grown children will want to visit you more and more.

Between her separated parents and my separated parents, we have four different families we are supposed to visit on major holidays. That doesn't bother my dad. He is so great. He tells us not to worry about seeing him at Christmas. He says he understands it is stressful. He would rather get with us for Martin Luther King weekend, when we all have Monday off. We meet at a neat place and have a couple of really relaxing days. We like that better than all of the other places we feel forced to go. We like visiting him more than anyone else. He makes it fun.

***

She is finally grown. Over twenty-one. Out of the house. But, college tuition will cause her to have debt the size of a house note. She'll never get out from under it. She cannot afford insurance AND go to school.

***

- **REFEREE'S RULE:** Do not be a holiday hog. Give it up and you will get more.

- **REFEREE'S RULE:** Good parents always encourage their children to succeed. When the child is college or trade school bound, parents should help with tuition. Insist they work while in school. Make them go to a cheaper state university if you must. Finally, do not let them be saddled with thousands of dollars worth of college or trade school loan debt if you can possibly help it.

- **LEGAL TIP:** Help your adult kids stay on health insurance and car insurance until they can get it themselves.

- **PRACTICAL TIP:** The more you give, the more you get.

- **TALKING TIP:** "I'll love you forever."

The Single Parent Referee
Appendices

This is **your** workbook. Each appendix ties to a specific chapter in the book. Make this work for you. Answer as much as you can and save it in a safe, confidential place. Update as often as you need to. It is up to you how you use this workbook. You can print out your workbook pages if you want to hand write it, and you can go to our website, www.singleparentreferee.com for resources and tips.

APPENDIX A

YOUR STORY (Chapter One)
Who are you? Where are you right now?

1. What are your strengths and weaknesses as a person and as a parent? This is your best and worst stuff.
Examples: "I have lots of energy."
"I can stroll with a baby for hours."
"I can coach soccer or baseball."
"I am a good cook."
"I am great with animals."
"I have a bad temper and no patience."
"I get bored and annoyed easily."

2. What do you like to do in your free time? With your child, then without your child. Examples: Go to the playground. Go to movies. Watch television. Watch sports. Hang out with friends.

3. Are you happy with your job/career choice? Have you had setbacks? Examples:
"I am still in school, but with the wrong major."
"My job went out of business."
"I really do not want to work."

4. What do you want to be doing in five years? Ten years? Examples: Own a business. Finish nursing school. Get a college degree. Get licensed as an electrician.

5. What will it take for you to make your goal? Examples: Go back to school. Pay off debts or student loans.

6. What changes do you intend to make on the career front? How and when? Is this realistic? Example: "I want to go to law school, but I made bad grades."

7. Is your housing stable? Is it a good place for your child? Does he or she have a room? His/her own bed? Toys?

8. Who do you live with? Is this good for your child? Will this person help you reach your goals?

9. Have there been any domestic violence scenes with you or the other parent?

10. Have the police ever been called to your house for fighting? Should they have been called?

11. Who is your support network? List each person in your network by name and phone number.

12. What are you most proud of?

13. How many years have you been involved with the other parent?

14. How many children do you have? How many does the other parent have?

15. What bothers you most about parenting? What is the main problem involving the other parent?

16. Can this be fixed or must you learn to live with it?
Examples: "She is married to someone else."
"He is in prison for the next five years."
"She picks a fight at every visitation drop off."
"She never gets her to school on time."

17. Do you have bitterness or resentment you cannot get over? What and why? (Use extra paper if necessary.)
Examples: "He or she used me, abused me, mistreated me, lied to me."

18. Do you want the other parent involved a lot? A little or not at all? Is this with you or with the child? Do YOU really want the other parent back? Examples: "We can co-parent this child apart." Or, "I never want to see him/her again." Or, "I really want to get back together with the other parent."

19. Have you caused hurt or mistrust that needs to be cleared up? How?

20. Have you said things that have caused major problems?
Example: "I told him he was not the dad, that his best friend was the baby's dad. It was not true."

21. Is there a negative pattern about your life that needs work? Example: "I always get involved with people at work and it messes up the job."

22. What are the really good things going on with your kids? Example: "They are doing great in school."

23. How does the rest of the family fit into the picture? Example: "My parents are very, very helpful/critical/unhelpful."

24. Is your childcare good? Is your child happy?

25. Keep writing the rest of your story.

APPENDIX B

What Do You Really Want? (Chapter Two)

1. **Describe in detail what parenting time/visitation schedule you want regarding your child and the other parent or his/her family.**

2. **List what you think you want to DO with your child. How much time do you want to spend with your child? Now? In the future?**
   Remember those three year milestones.

3. **When do you need a break?**
   (For example, every Friday night, or maybe Sunday afternoons?)

4. **How involved do you want to be with their activities? Really?**

5. **What educational/child care decisions do you want to make?**
For example, what school should your child attend? Are you prepared to help transport and help pay?

6. **Look ahead at least one milestone (three years) and see how you think things might change. What school changes might there be? Will you or the other parent be engaged or married?**

7. **What holidays are important to you and your family?**
Consider if you work all Christmas and need help during the holidays.

8. **What family events matter to you and your family?**
For example, claim the week of your family reunion if it is important to you that your child be part of that celebration.

9. **What is your work schedule? School schedule? Study schedule? When will it change?**

10. What is your child's schedule?

11. Does your child have any unique needs?

12. What is the other parent's schedule?

13. What family members are available and dependable?

APPENDIX C
Your Issues (Chapter Two)

1. List your issues with the other parent.
Write down what hurts or angers you the most.

2. What religious faith will this child follow? What are your options? What and why? Who does it matter to the most?

3. What school/daycare will this child attend? Who deals with the teachers? What parent will the school call first? Can you afford a private school? Is there a family tradition anywhere? Does it matter? Are there issues?

4. What values do you have that are different from the other parent?
(This could take pages!)

5. What role will grandparents play, and can you depend on them to play fair?

APPENDIX D
Just the Facts (Chapter Two)

1. List names, schools, jobs, housing.

- Write down full names and detailed information about each child, the other parent, any significant stepparent or other ex, and their children. This even includes custody information about the other parent's other children. It may surprise you that this information is important, but an ex-stepparent can be very significant. What conflict did the prior spouse/lover have before you?

- Get detailed school and daycare information about each child.

- Get information about your current job, and also about your previous jobs. You'll need information about the other parent's jobs, too.

- Get the name of a character witness at your current job. This is someone who can verify that you have a good boss who understands your parental issues.

- Get detailed information about where you live, the neighborhood, and who lives there along with the same information about the other parent.

2. List Medical History.

- Get detailed health insurance and medical information on yourself, your children, the other parent, and others. Beware of HIPAA, health information privacy federal laws that make it difficult to get those records. Make sure you do not violate those laws. In general, you are entitled to medical records on yourself and your children, but you need a court order to get anyone else's, UNLESS, they give it to you or leave it out for you to see. That is why it is important to permanently save and store this information when you have proper access to it.

3. List Mental Health History.

- Outline all mental health history. This family history is different from medical history and much more sensitive. First, identify the mental health issues; second, try to list what triggers problems; third, what can be done to avoid the problems.

- A critical element of mental health history is substance abuse. Addiction problems to alcohol, pills and illegal drugs impact your kids. List it all.

4. List Criminal History.

List any arrests, dates, locations and outcomes.

5. List Non-criminal Legal History.

List non-criminal problems like bankruptcy, divorces, and paternity/DNA tests.

6. List Significant Dates.

List wedding dates, separation dates, moving dates, etc. Many of them you may already have listed in the above categories.

7. List Crisis Events.

Anything from a car accident to a hurricane to a death in the family can place enormous stress on children. List the details.

8. List Military Issues.

If someone in the family is in the military, and away on active duty, this can impact the kids. List who, what, when and where.

APPENDIX E
The Changes (Chapter Eight)

List how you will, would, should or have handled the following:

- One or both parents get married.

- Other children are born or come with the marriage.

- Children become teenagers or adults.

- Somebody loses his/her job.

- A grandparent or close relative dies.

- Someone moves.

APPENDIX F

The Money (Chapter Ten)

1. Here is what really counts for child support worksheets.

- How much time do you spend with your child? Count actual 24 hour days/nights blocks.

- What is everyone's present income.

- What is the cost of the daycare/afterschool/babysitter the custodial parent needs to go to work? Who pays it?

- Who pays for health insurance, and how much is it?

- Are there any really high medical costs?

- What other children live in each parent's home?

- How much do you *actually* pay in child support for other children?

2. Also list the following:

- Family contributions

- School expenses

- Private school tuition, if both parents signed the private school contract

- Recurring medical bills that are not large

- Reason for no visitation (What if the parent with custody has interfered?)

- Extracurricular activities of the child, which cost extra and are paid by one parent

3. List what you know about the following:

- His/her past income

- His/her ability to earn

- His/her education

- His/her reason for a decrease in income

- His/her reason for changing employment

APPENDIX G
Parenting Time (Chapter Eleven)

1. Who will the child actually visit? In whose house?

2. What will your child will be doing?

3. Who are the neighbors and friends, what overnight friends visit?

4. When will the child go and when will the child return to you?

5. How will transportation be handled?

6. What is or will be the regular phone contact, private communication by e-mail or text when the child is staying with the other parent.

APPENDIX H

"Preparing for a Custody Hearing (Chapter Twelve)

To make sure you are prepared whenever you might have a custody hearing, always keep and constantly update a journal of:

- All available family

- Child's relationship with the family or the one who wants custody

- That person's track record as a parent

- The physical and mental health of the parties

- Ability to support the child

- Motive for wanting custody

- Sex and age of parties seeking custody

- Home environment based upon social worker's home study

- The child's preference, if he or she is mature

- Report of Guardian Ad Litem, GAL, (the court-appointed attorney for the child) or a Court Appointed Special Advocate, CASA.

About the Author

Claudia Haltom sat on the Memphis and Shelby County Juvenile Court bench for 17 years, hearing cases and ruling on family law and juvenile matters. She judged custody, visitation, paternity and child support cases. She has been a practicing attorney and judge for over 30 years. After getting her B.S. in journalism, she graduated from the University of Tennessee College of Law. Now, in her retirement, she is the CEO for A Step Ahead Foundation, Inc.

For more information,
www.singleparentreferee.com

**Find more books from
Keith Publications, LLC
At**

www.keithpublications.com

CPSIA information can be obtained at www.ICGtesting.com
Printed in the USA
BVOW04s1134271013

334775BV00005B/31/P